WHY
are there more women than men?

WHY
are there more women than men?

The brand-name products mentioned in this publication are trademarks or service marks of their respective companies.

Copyright © 2010 Publications International, Ltd. All rights reserved. This book may not be reproduced or quoted in whole or in part by any means whatsoever without written permission from:

Louis Weber, CEO
Publications International, Ltd.
7373 North Cicero Avenue
Lincolnwood, Illinois 60712

Permission is never granted for commercial purposes.

ISBN-13: 978-1-60553-382-7
ISBN-10: 1-60553-382-3

Manufactured in USA

8 7 6 5 4 3 2 1

Contents

Why are there more women than men? 13
Why did women start wearing high heels? 15
Why are fire engines red? 16
Why are skunks so stinky? 18
Why are some motorcycles called choppers? 19
Why aren't hamburgers made of ham? 21
Why did ancient Egyptians shave their eyebrows? 23
Why did John Hancock sign his name so big on the Declaration of Independence? 24
Why isn't a boxing ring round? 26
Why don't they make mouse-flavored cat food? 27
Why is Australia considered a continent instead of an island? 28
Why does squinting help you see? 29
Why do you have to be quiet when a golfer is swinging? 31
Why does fruitcake keep so long? 33
Why did Abraham Lincoln have an air corps? 34
Why are there stripes on bowling pins? 36
Why do crows always take the most direct route? 37
Why does it cost more to insure a red car? 39

Why are salaries a taboo topic? 40
Why can't we remember much of anything
that happened before the age of three? 42
Why do zebras have stripes? 44
Why are ineligible college athletes called redshirts? 46
Why is it good to be a wise man but not a wise guy? 47
Why would anyone buy an aluminum Christmas tree? 49
Why do bees die after they sting? 50
Why do your ears pop in an airplane? 52
Why does time seem to move faster as you get older? 53
Why is a marathon 26.2 miles? 54
Why was smallpox so deadly for Indians,
but not Europeans? 56
Why does the color red anger bulls? 58
Why don't Grape-Nuts contain grapes or nuts? 59
Why are there only two sexes? 61
Why is Thanksgiving on Thursday? 63
Why is America called America? 65
Why do doctors have such lousy handwriting? 67
Why doesn't water in a water tower freeze? 68
Why do onions make you cry? 69
Why do professors wear blazers with elbow patches? 71
Why do the Dallas Cowboys and Detroit Lions
always play on Thanksgiving? 72
Why does Australia have so many poisonous snakes? 74
Why are vitamins good for us? 75
Why do cats always land on their feet? 77

Why is IBM referred to as Big Blue?	79
Why would anyone want to be the devil's advocate?	80
Why didn't the Vikings stay in North America?	82
Why do bruises turn different colors while they're healing?	83
Why do doughnuts have holes?	84
Why is Kansas City in Missouri and Missouri City in Texas?	86
Why do drive-up ATMs have Braille?	87
Why do Space Shuttle astronauts wear parachutes?	88
Why does a rattlesnake's tail rattle?	90
Why do some people dream in black and white?	91
Why is there a dropped-third-strike rule in baseball?	93
Why do we have earwax?	95
Why can Sherpas exist at higher altitudes than anyone else?	96
Why are objects in my car's side-view mirror closer than they appear?	98
Why are Persian rugs so expensive?	99
Why do people shake hands?	101
Why isn't Scotland Yard in Scotland?	102
Why do traffic lights use the colors red, yellow, and green?	103
Why do you get "brain freeze" from eating or drinking something cold?	105
Why does the Leaning Tower of Pisa lean?	106
Why aren't people covered in hair like other primates?	108

Why is a white flag a symbol of surrender? ... 110
Why don't school buses have seatbelts? ... 111
Why is the sky blue? ... 113
Why do the Amish keep telephones outside their homes? ... 114
Why do snakes shed their skin? ... 116
Why do you remember some things and forget other things? ... 117
Why does Swiss cheese have holes? ... 119
Why are Mexican jumping beans so jumpy? ... 121
Why do body parts "fall asleep"? ... 123
Why are guinea pigs used in so many experiments? ... 124
Why are most plants green? ... 126
Why do speedometers list speeds faster than you can legally drive? ... 127
Why do doctors hit your knee with a hammer? ... 129
Why are some women called "catty"? ... 130
Why does a turkey have light and dark meat? ... 132
Why is Chicago called the Windy City? ... 133
Why is the U.S. presidential election held on a Tuesday in November? ... 135
Why does a nuclear explosion form a mushroom cloud? ... 136
Why do we put candles on a birthday cake? ... 137
Why do toddlers get so many ear infections? ... 139
Why is the heart associated with love? ... 140
Why is yawning contagious? ... 141
Why do radio and TV station call letters begin with W or K? ... 143

Why do parents give their kids names
that no one can pronounce or spell?......................... 145
Why does a seashell sound like the ocean? 147
Why do you always wake up just before
you die in a dream?.. 147
Why do round pizzas come in square boxes? 149
Why are reflections in a mirror reversed?.................... 151
Why is the day after Thanksgiving called Black Friday? .. 152
Why doesn't the United States use the metric system? ... 154
Why do college football coaches have
armed state troopers with them on the sideline? 156
Why are Democrats on the left and
Republicans on the right? 157
Why is it called a honeymoon?..................................... 159
Why do phone numbers on TV shows
and in movies start with 555? 160
Why do they call it the Dark Ages? 161
Why do trees lose their leaves? 163
Why does the American flag have stripes? 164
Why are people afraid of clowns?................................. 165
Why do marathon runners wrap themselves
in foil after a race? 167
Why do grapes spark in the microwave? 168
Why can't you teach an old dog new tricks? 170
Why is coffee called "joe"?.. 171
Why hasn't anyone found a cure for
the common cold?... 173

Why do baseball managers and coaches
wear uniforms instead of street clothes?........................ 174
Why are some chicken eggs white and others brown? ... 176
Why did doctors perform lobotomies? 177
Why can't you tickle yourself? 180
Why is it always the other guy who has an accent?........ 181
Why isn't anyone ever smiling in old photographs? 182
Why is it called rush hour when traffic is the slowest? ... 184
Why do horseshoes bring good luck?.............................. 185
Why do old newspapers turn yellow? 187
Why do computers crash?.. 188
Why do pregnant women crave pickles?........................ 190
Why does garlic give you bad breath? 192
Why do so many country names end in "-stan"?............ 193
Why is everything more painful when it's cold? 195
Why is a football shaped that way?................................. 196
Why aren't all gas caps on the same side of the car?...... 198
Why do cows lie down before it rains? 199
Why do old churches have steeples?............................... 200
Why do dogs lick people?.. 202
Why is it harder to lose weight as you age?.................... 202
Why can't the government just print more money to
stimulate the economy? 204
Why do firehouses keep Dalmatians? 206
Why do mattresses come with tags that say,
"Do Not Remove Under Penalty of Law"? 207
Why is a pirate flag called a Jolly Roger? 208

Why do mosquitoes bite some people more than others? 210
Why do golfers hate to putt? 212
Why don't penguins and polar bears get frostbite? 213
Why does an orchestra conductor need a baton? 215
Why do we give names to hurricanes and cyclones? 217
Why are three straight bowling strikes called a Turkey? 219
Why do fruits and vegetables change colors as they ripen? 220
Why do newer car models have letters and numbers instead of names? 222
Why does gin taste like pine needles? 224
Why does mercury rise or fall depending on the temperature? 225
Why would one person try to get another's goat? 226
Why does organic milk last longer than regular milk? 228
Why do we see our breath on a cold day? 229
Why doesn't your stomach digest itself? 230
Why are school buses yellow? 231
Why do most sports go counterclockwise? 233
Why do we say "head over heels in love"? 235
Why do we cross our fingers for good luck? 236
Why do we sweat? 238
Why do people dress up their pets? 239
Why do airplane seats need to be "fully upright" for takeoff and landing? 241

Why is red wine served at room temperature
and white wine chilled?.. 242
Why do we carve jack-o'-lanterns? 243
Why do we have to "face the music"? 246
Why does the U.S. president pardon a turkey
each Thanksgiving?... 247
Why should I mind my P's and Q's?................................ 248
Why do we tip some service people but not others? 250
Why does reading in the car make you sick? 252
Why do we trick-or-treat? 253
Why is salt both good and bad for you? 255
Why do parties always end up in the kitchen? 256
Why do ostriches stick their heads in the sand? 257
Why does K stand for strikeout? 259
Why don't we run out of water?...................................... 260
Why is the bald eagle the U.S. national bird? 262
Why do AM stations broadcast farther
than FM stations?.. 264
Why are we supposed to remember the Alamo? 265
Why does ninety-three octane gas cost more
than eighty-seven octane gas?... 267

CONTRIBUTORS 270

Q: Why are there more women than men?

A: Men are often referred to as the stronger sex, but women definitely outperform them when it comes to longevity. According to total population estimates in the CIA's *The World Factbook*, women outnumber men in most countries. Gender ratio estimates for 2008 say that there are 0.97 males for every female in the United States, 0.91 males for every female in Monaco, and 0.86 males for every female in the Ukraine.

Yet in newborn populations, men have a slight edge. There are about 107 boys born for every one hundred girls worldwide. If you're wondering where the boys are, they're not all having sex-change operations. It turns out that throughout different stages of life, men face higher mortality rates than women.

For example, between the ages of fifteen and twenty-four, men are four to five times more likely to die than women. Marianne Legato, a specialist in gender-specific medicine at Columbia University, says this is because men—particularly adolescents—are biologically more inclined toward risky behavior.

Researchers often refer to this increase in reckless and violent behavior as a full-on "testosterone storm." It gets guys in this pubescent age group into a whole lot of trouble—mainly death by car accident, homicide, suicide, or drowning.

After the age of twenty-four, the mortality rate for men and women tends to even out. But beyond the age of fifty, it's all downhill for the misters. Research conducted at Harvard University Medical School shows that from the ages of fifty-five to sixty-four, men are once again more likely to die than women. This time, the deaths are often from tobacco and alcohol use and heart disease, in addition to car accidents and suicide.

In her book, *Why Men Die First*, Legato says that across national and cultural boundaries, men die an average of seven years earlier than women. Over a period of time, that slowly alters overall gender ratios.

In the United States, there are 1.05 males for every female in the under-fifteen age category, but only 0.73 males for every female in the sixty-five and older category. However, the gender gap is widest among those who live one hundred years or longer. Worldwide, female centenarians outnumber their male counterparts by a ratio of nine to one.

Ladies looking for love after hitting that century mark might consider a move to Qatar in the Middle East. In the sixty-five and older group, there are 2.92 males for every female. Who knows? You might nab yourself a nice spring chicken.

Q Why did women start wearing high heels?

A "High heels were invented by a woman who had been kissed on the forehead," quipped twentieth-century American writer Christopher Morley. He may have been on to something.

Though the precise history of the high heel is somewhat up in the air, it's believed that the first woman to strut in stilettos was a particularly petite gal named Catherine de Medici. Yes, that Catherine de Medici. In 1533, this member of the influential Italian Renaissance family commissioned a Florentine artist to craft a very special pair of shoes for her forthcoming nuptials to Henry, the rather tall duke of Orleans and the son of France's King Francis I.

Like any bride, Catherine wanted to make a grand entrance at her wedding. But impressing the Royal Court of France was a pretty tall order for a girl who was less than five feet tall. That she was merely fourteen years old perhaps added to the pressure.

The Italian artisan consulted by Catherine came through with the perfect pair of shoes to temporarily elevate her stature. Indeed, upon arriving in France, Catherine's higher heels caused quite the stir among the ladies of the French court. They immediately became en vogue and went on to become a fashion staple.

Today, designer heels from such names as Jimmy Choo, Stuart Weitzman, and Christian Louboutin are essential to the with-it woman's accessory arsenal. They make her look taller and promote the illusion of slender, toned legs. And wearing high heels also pushes the chest forward and the butt rearward, which accentuates the feminine form—or, at least, the male ideal of the feminine form.

Most women will confess that while high heels look good, darn, they hurt. Got blisters, corns, hammertoes, or bunions to go along with those sexy spikes? Curse Catherine de Medici. You'd be in fashionable company; the French never really liked the little squirt, anyway.

Q Why are fire engines red?

A Give a youngster a box of crayons, ask for a drawing of a fire engine, and watch those little fingers reach for red. Kids know that red is the right color for a fire truck—it's adults who don't always agree.

Precisely why fire engines are red is lost in the smoky recesses of history. Experts from such agencies as the U.S. Fire Administration and the National Fire Protection Association (NFPA) cite theories, but even they admit that no one knows for sure. Most conjecture leads to the nineteenth century, when firefighting in America was an ad hoc pursuit and competition between public, private, and volunteer brigades was fierce. Crews would race each other to a blaze, and the first group on the scene took control. Sometimes it was to secure a claim on any fire insurance money; often it was just for the glory. The rivalry extended to uniforms and equipment: The brighter and more elaborate, the more prestigious. Not only was red the shade most identified with fire, it was the most regal and expensive color with which to paint the firefighting apparatus. Thus was born a tradition.

Another theory holds that red became the accepted color for safety reasons in the early twentieth century, when most automobiles were black and red was thought to stand out best in traffic. Indeed, the visibility of fire trucks to other motorists remains a matter of grave importance. NFPA records show a steady increase in the number of collisions involving fire emergency vehicles going to or from a blaze. In 2006, for instance, there were 16,020 such collisions, resulting in 1,250 injuries and the deaths of nineteen firefighters.

Safety concerns once led to a flirtation with alternatives to fire-engine red. The movement was fueled by research suggesting that hues of yellow or lime are more visible to the human eye, particularly at dusk or nighttime since they are more reflective. Indeed, support for a switch to yellow, lime green, or white from red was strong in the 1970s and 1980s. But subsequent analysis revealed little difference in the number of collisions.

It turns out that color has virtually no effect on how visible a fire truck is to motorists, but lighting and reflective surfaces do. The NFPA never had a requirement for fire truck color, but in 1991 it established new standards that increased the number and size of emergency lights and specified their brightness and location. It also added standards for the size, placement, and color of reflective striping. Though the Federal Aviation Administration stuck with lime-yellow for airport emergency vehicles, municipal fire departments have trended back to the color red. The government's Occupational Safety and Health Administration also favors red in its standards.

Most firefighters couldn't be happier. They say that the public never really associated lime with fire trucks, and anything other than red somehow bucked a proud tradition. Any kid with a crayon in his hand could have told you as much.

Q: Why are skunks so stinky?

A: Oh, so you smell like a bed of roses? But seriously, skunks have earned their odiferous reputation through their marvelous ability to make other things stink to high heaven.

All eleven species of skunk have stinky spray housed in their anal glands. However, as dog owners can attest, skunks aren't the only animals to have anal glands filled with terrible-smelling substances. Opossums are particularly bad stinkers; an opossum will empty its anal glands when "playing dead" to help it smell like a rotting corpse.

While no animal's anal glands are remotely fragrant, skunks' pack an especially pungent stench. This is because skunks use their spray as a defense mechanism. And they have amazing range: Skunks have strong muscles surrounding the glands, which allow them to spray sixteen feet or more on a good day.

A skunk doesn't want to stink up the place. It does everything in its power to warn predators before it douses its target with *eau de skunk*. A skunk will jump up and down, stomp its feet, hiss, and lift its tail in the air, all in the hope that the predator will realize that it's dealing with a skunk and go away. A skunk only does what it does best when it feels it has no choice. Then it releases the nauseating mix of thiols (chemicals that contain super-stinky sulfur), which makes whatever it hits undateable for the foreseeable future. Skunks have enough "stink juice" stored up for about five or six sprays; after they empty their anal glands, it takes up to ten days to replenish the supply.

Being sprayed by a skunk is an extremely unpleasant experience. Besides the smell, the spray from a skunk can cause nausea and temporary blindness. Bobcats, foxes, coyotes, and badgers usually only hunt skunk if they are really, really hungry. Only the great horned owl makes skunk a regular snack—and the fact that the great horned owl barely has a sense of smell probably has a lot to do with it.

Should you find yourself on the receiving end of a skunk shower, your best deodorizer is alkaline hydrogen peroxide. But unless you startle a skunk (which is possible, since the critter doesn't have keen eyesight), you'll probably have plenty of chances not to get sprayed. You and a skunk have a lot in common: You don't want to get sprayed, and the skunk doesn't want to spray you.

Q: Why are some motorcycles called choppers?

A: Nothing beats twisting open the throttle with miles of dry road ahead, but chewing on biker lingo is surely part of the appeal of life on two wheels. And no word in the vroom-vroom vocabulary is more widely used—or more often misused—than "chopper."

It's come to identify almost any motorcycle that strays from strictly stock. The term owes much of its currency to popular television programs such as *American Chopper* and *Monster Garage*, the show that catapulted host Jesse G. James and his West Coast Choppers shop into the public eye.

But a bike must do more than deviate from factory specs to be a proper chopper, and most of those TV "choppers" more correctly fit the definition of a custom motorcycle. The true chopper grows from the belief that less is more, and is rooted in a time when motorcycles first connected with the romantic rebel in us.

It was just after World War II. Thousands of young soldiers returned to America from overseas, wiser for their military experience and maybe a little impatient with the routines of peacetime. The most restless among them saw an opportunity for low-cost excitement in bargain-priced war-surplus motorcycles. These were commonly sturdy Harley-Davidsons, but sturdy meant heavy—and heavy meant slow. Engine modifications helped, but to go really fast, these bikes had to lose weight.

Innovators started by removing components that were not purely functional, such as front fenders, heavy seats, extraneous gauges, and lights. Rear fenders were retained to protect riders from road spray, but were trimmed to the minimum, or bobbed. These early modified bikes were, in fact, dubbed "bobbers."

But they were still too heavy to satisfy the most radical speed demons, who found the lightness they desired by cutting off—or chopping away—any part of the motorcycle they deemed unnecessary. The bikes they created were loud, personal, and provocative. And quite naturally, they came to be called choppers.

The form evolved in the 1960s, with stock frames carefully chopped up, lowered, and expertly reassembled around hopped-up engines. Orthodox choppers never strayed from the goal of going fast, though looking radical was always part of the game; some builders expressed this with angled forks that pushed the front wheel far ahead.

Chopper style was cool, and the term was evocative, so it was the natural launching pad for a new wave of modified motorcycles with artsy frames, chromed accessories, and other filigree whose primary purpose was aesthetic. These can be breathtakingly beautiful customs, but they are seldom bona fide choppers.

Q Why aren't hamburgers made of ham?

A If you remember the jingle for the McDonald's Big Mac, the ingredients list for the classic American burger is clear: "Two all-beef patties, special sauce, lettuce, cheese, pickles, onions on a sesame seed bun." Nowhere is there a mention of pork products. How, then, did ham get into your burger?

This is more a question of etymology than gastronomy. Literally translated, "hamburger" means "from Hamburg." And Hamburg, Germany, is exactly where favorites like the Whopper, Slyder, and Quarter Pounder got their humble beginnings.

Before we get ahead of ourselves, let's travel back to the Middle Ages and examine the origins of shredded beef. It's widely accepted that the Mongolian and Turkic tribes of this period were the first to shred low-quality beef into smaller pieces. They ate this tough beef raw, and shredding it made the meat more edible and digestible. You might know these nomadic tribes by another name: the Tatars, or Tartars. Yes, they're the guys who gave us what came to be known as "steak tartare."

The Russian Tatars brought the concept of shredded beef to Germany sometime before the seventeenth century. The Germans added their own twist to the tartare recipe, flavoring the beef with regional spices and sometimes even cooking it. Over time, this meal of pounded beef became quite common, particularly among the poorer classes in Hamburg. In and around this seaport town, the beef patty became known as "Hamburg steak."

How did a slab of seasoned, minced beef from Hamburg make its way to so many restaurant drive-thrus and backyard barbecues in America? It's believed that Hamburg steak came to the United States along with the many German immigrants aboard the German Hamburg-Amerika Line of the mid- to late eighteen hundreds. Back then, travel from Europe to the States took weeks, and the salted, sometimes smoked beefsteaks were ideal for long sea voyages.

Once in the United States, German immigrants continued to prepare the Hamburg steak. It began showing up on restaurant menus by the 1880s, and by 1902 the popular *Mrs. Rorer's New Cook Book* featured a recipe of ground beef mixed with onion and pepper, which closely resembles the burger as we know it today.

Around the beginning of the twentieth century, Hamburg steak acquired two pieces of bread or toast—and a new name. There is great debate over who prepared the first all-American hamburger on a bun. We can safely rule out at least one person: Colonel Sanders.

Q Why did ancient Egyptians shave their eyebrows?

A Shaving away all body hair, including eyebrows, was part of an elaborate daily purification ritual that was practiced by Pharaoh and his priests.

The ancient Egyptians believed that everything in their lives—health, good crops, victory, prosperity—depended on keeping their gods happy, so one of Pharaoh's duties was to enter a shrine and approach a special statue of a god three times a day, every day. Each time he visited the shrine, Pharaoh washed the statue, anointed it with oil, and dressed it in fresh linen.

Because Pharaoh was a busy guy, high-ranking priests often performed this duty for him. But whether it was Pharaoh or a priest doing it, the person had to bathe himself and shave his eyebrows beforehand.

Shaving the eyebrows was also a sign of mourning, even among commoners. The Greek historian Herodotus, who traveled and wrote in the fifth century BC, said that everyone in an ancient Egyptian household would shave his or her eyebrows following the natural death of a pet cat. For dogs, he reported, the household members would shave their heads and all of their body hair as well.

Herodotus was known to repeat some wild stories in his books—for instance, he reported that serpents with bat-like wings flew from Arabia into Egypt and were killed in large numbers by ibises. Herodotus claimed he actually saw heaps of these serpent skeletons. So you might want to take his eyebrow-shaving claim with a grain of salt... and a pinch of catnip.

Q: Why did John Hancock sign his name so big on the Declaration of Independence?

A: Poor John Hancock—he was the president of the Continental Congress as the United States sprang to life, and a nine-term governor of Massachusetts. Heck, he even graduated from Harvard.

But what's his legacy? Penmanship. If he had known this would be his ignominious fate, perhaps he wouldn't have scrawled his name so largely on the Declaration of Independence or added that fancy loop to the "k." But he did write that big, and he did add that loop—so now we're forced to listen to some waiter quip, "Just give me your John Hancock," every fifth time we pay with a credit card at a restaurant.

One of the reasons Hancock's signature is so enormous is that he, as president of the Continental Congress, was the first to sign the Declaration of Independence. Hancock had plenty of real estate, and he used it. But goodness gracious, there were fifty-five other signatures that needed to be added. Leave some room for everyone else, guy.

Still, it wasn't necessarily a case of a man doing something simply because he could. Hancock felt that a big signature was important. Signing such a document did two things: First, it told American colonists and the rest of the world why the Congress felt it was necessary to break away from Great Britain. Second, by creating the Declaration of Independence, the congressional members were directly insulting England's King George III, a treasonous act that could lead to hanging. Hancock believed that a bold sweep of his feathered quill would instill confidence and courage into his fellow colonial delegates, and into everyone else who read the document.

It's been said that after signing his name, Hancock defiantly exclaimed, "There, I guess King George will be able to read that!" or "The British ministry can read that name without spectacles; let them double the reward for my head!" Sure, and George Washington never told a lie. In all likelihood, Hancock never made such a boast—there simply wasn't the audience for it. Only one other person was present when Hancock signed the Declaration of Independence: Charles Thomson, the secretary of the Continental Congress, who claimed that Hancock never uttered such words. Besides, saying something that grandiose with just one other person in the room would have been, well, weird.

The delegates voted to ratify the Declaration of Independence on the night of July 4, 1776, but they did not sign it. (Now, go out and use that piece of info to win a bar bet!) The first version was printed, copied, signed by Hancock and Thomson, and distributed to political and military leaders for their review. On July 19, the Congress ordered that the document be "fairly engrossed on parchment," a fancy way of saying officially written. On August 2, the final version was ready to be signed. Hancock signed first, putting his John, er, his name in the middle of the document below the text. As was the custom, others started signing their names below Hancock's.

Not everyone whose name is on the Declaration of Independence was present that day. Signatures were added in the coming days, weeks, months, and years. The last person to sign was Thomas McKean, in 1781. And you just know that when McKean saw what little room there was for his signature, he thought, "[Bleeping] Hancock!"

Q Why isn't a boxing ring round?

A Boxing has been around for ages because, when you get down to it, humans like to pummel each other. The ancient Greeks were the ones who decided to make it into a legitimate sport: Boxing was introduced as an Olympic event in 688 BC. The competitors wrapped pieces of soft leather around their hands and proceeded to fight.

The Romans took it a little further, adding bits of metal to the leather. No wonder those guys ruled most of the known world for so long!

Fast forward to England in the eighteenth century. Boxing was popular—and it was violent. The fighters battled each other inside a ring of rope that was lined with—and sometimes held up by—spectators. That's right, a *ring*. These spectators couldn't be counted on to be sober and often raucously crowded the boxers—the rope ring would get smaller and smaller until the onlookers were practically on top of the fighters. Often the spectators would have a go at it with the boxers themselves.

Understandably, the fighters got a bit testy about the situation. Jack Broughton, a heavyweight champion, came up with a set of rules to protect his fellow boxers in 1743. His plan included a chalked-off square inside which the boxers would fight. Event organizers attached rope to stakes that were pounded into the ground, which prevented the fighting area from changing sizes and from being invaded. Why a square? Because it was easy to make.

Broughton's rules were eventually revised to formalize the square shape. By 1853, the rules stated that matches had to take place in a twenty-four-foot square "ring" that was enclosed by ropes. That, good reader, is the origin of what boxing aficionados call "the squared circle."

Q: Why don't they make mouse-flavored cat food?

A: There's no denying that cats have a thing for mice. It begins with the thrill of the chase, and if all goes as planned (for the cat), it ends with the satisfaction of downing a wiggling bundle of fur and bones, squeak and all.

It's feline instinct, but it's not entirely unlike the way you hit the couch, reach for the remote control, turn on the television, enjoy the thrill of a cop-show chase, and stuff your face with those special potato chips—the cheap, greasy ones that you'd never admit to loving. What's the similarity? For both the cat and for you, it's the easiest thing that's available because it's right in front of you. It's low-hanging fruit, so to speak.

If a mouse is so brazen or so foolish as to wander into Tabby's territory, the cat is going to make entertainment and a snack out of it. If that television is just going to sit there and if those chips are simply going to take up cupboard space, your best option is to make entertainment and a snack out of them. You get the general idea, right?

A cat would rather dine on, say, a tuna, but there aren't any flopping around your family rec room. Felines don't prefer to eat mice; they eat them because they're convenient prey. Remember, cats also dine on bugs—and you don't see bug-flavored cat food at your local pet store, do you?

Q Why is Australia considered a continent instead of an island?

A In grammar school, some of us were far more interested in the "social" aspect of social studies than the "studies" part. Nevertheless, everyone can recite the continents: Africa, Asia, Europe, South America, North America, Australia, and... some other one. What gives with Australia? Why is it a continent? Shouldn't it be an island?

It most certainly is an island (the world's largest) and so much more. Australia is the only land mass on Earth to be considered an island, a country, and a continent.

Australia is by far the smallest continent, leading one to wonder why it is labeled a continent at all when other large islands, such as Greenland, are not. The answer lies in plate tectonics, the geologic theory explaining how Earth's land masses got to where they are today. According to plate tectonic theory, all of Earth's continents once formed a giant land mass known as Pangaea. Though Pangaea was one mass, it actually comprised several distinct pieces of land known as plates.

Over millions of years, at roughly the speed of your hair growth, these plates shifted, drifting apart from one another until they reached their current positions. Some plates stayed connected, such as South America and North America, while others moved off into a remote corner like a punished child, such as Australia. (It's no wonder Australia was first used by the British as a prison colony.) Because Australia is one of these plates—while Greenland is part of the North American plate—it gets the honor of being called a continent.

All of this debate might ultimately seem rather silly. Some geologists maintain that in 250 million years, the continents will move back into one large mass called Pangaea Ultima. Australia will merge with Southeast Asia—and social studies tests will get a whole lot easier.

Q: Why does squinting help you see?

 Most of us don't think much about squinting. It's a highly underrated bodily function—it doesn't receive nearly the amount of pub that, say, belching does. But if we couldn't squint, much of the pageantry of life would elude us. (Okay, that's a bit of an overstatement, but we're trying to get a point across here.)

Light comes into your eyes as individual rays from all directions. The front of each eye has a lens that bends these rays and redirects them onto your retina, which is located at the back of the eye. This focused light forms an image on the retina, in the same way the lens on a camera bends light rays to form an image on film (or on a charge-coupled device in a digital camera).

When everything is working precisely, the lens focuses the rays directly onto the retina, forming crisp images. But for many people, the process works less than ideally. The lens bends some rays in such ways that crisp images form slightly in front of or behind the retina, not directly on it.

As a result, things at certain distances appear blurry. This issue is most severe with rays that come into the eye at sharper angles (light from above or below your line of sight), because the lens bends those rays more than the ones that arrive straight on.

So how does squinting help to solve this pesky problem? It covers the top and bottom of your eye, thereby eliminating many of the rays that arrive at sharp angles; your lens receives only the head-on rays. Squinting also changes the shape of your eye, in kind of the same way that Lasik surgery does. All of this adds up to clearer images.

Basically, squinting acts as a filter—it blocks the peripheral information and allows only the good stuff to enter. So take a moment or two to praise this handy little visual aid. Without squinting, life would be a blurry mess. (Okay, we're exaggerating again, but you get the idea.)

Q: Why do you have to be quiet when a golfer is swinging?

A: At first blush, the answer seems obvious: So the golfer can concentrate. But it brings up subsequent questions: Why do golfers insist that they be allowed to concentrate when, say, football and baseball players do not? The answers have to do with the particular demands of golf and the particular social milieu in which it's been played for several centuries.

Let's start with the physical and mental demands. There is probably no other sport that requires such a combination of power and precision—of power applied precisely. Tiger Woods propels a full drive at about 150 miles per hour, yet he's envisioning a landing area that's not much more than ten yards wide, some 240 yards down the fairway.

If one part of Tiger's body moves more than a fraction of an inch in the wrong way while he swings, or if the timing of his swing is imprecise—he releases his wrists a fraction of a second too soon, say—the ball can travel thirty, forty, fifty yards or more off-target.

It's just as demanding on the green. Two hundred years ago, golf greens were as shaggy as a carpet. Now, the better the course, the shorter the greens are. At Augusta National Golf Club during the Masters Tournament, they are just a little more forgiving than linoleum. Tiger needs to control every nuance of the length, speed, and pace of his putting swing in order to prevent the ball from scurrying yards past the hole. This—like his drive—requires fantastic physical coordination, sensory sophistication, and concentration.

But not too much concentration. The hallmark of a hack golfer is his reliance on a mental checklist before every swing. "Head down, shoulder tucked, left arm straight..." Tiger has drilled these requisites into his unconscious mind—and into his muscles. But in order for that natural process to take place as programmed—in order to achieve the right combination of concentration and calm—he needs quiet. Tiger is so routinized, in fact, that he loses his temper when fans make unexpected noises or take pictures during his swing.

Maybe if golfers grew up amid bedlam, like football players do, they wouldn't mind the distractions. But they're accustomed to quiet. Which gets to the matter of tradition. For much of its history, golf has been a club sport. Clubs are laden with rules that seem arbitrary and stuffy to outsiders but make the social experience more meaningful for members. There are all sorts of formalities in golf clubs regarding gentlemanly behavior and the like, and these have extended to the course, where golfers go out of their way to observe them.

For example, the player who had the lowest score on the previous hole always tees off first on the next. If someone forgets and accidentally tees off out of turn, it's embarrassing, even among good friends. This powerful social component of golf colors every minute on the course, and keeping quiet during a golfer's swing is the most obligatory courtesy. So, as with almost everything in golf, there's more to this custom than meets the eyes...and ears.

Q: Why does fruitcake keep so long?

A: That's easy: It's loaded with booze. No mold can grow in that much alcohol. Fruitcakes start with fruit—fresh or dried—that is typically soaked for a week in port wine, bourbon, or dark rum. When the cake batter is mixed, a cup of whisky, brandy, or another equally potent liquor is likely to be one of the ingredients.

Alcohol is sometimes added even after the cake is baked. Some recipes call for the fruitcake to be sprinkled with brandy once a week for a month or more. If you don't want to go the sprinkling route, you can soak a towel in brandy and wrap it around the cake. A few old-fashioned cooks bake the cake with a cup placed in the middle in order to create a deep depression. When the cake cools, the depression is filled with brandy or rum, which soaks into the cake. This process can be repeated again and again as the cake absorbs each dose of alcohol.

Not every cook wants to get the family drunk on fruitcake. Some recipes leave the booze out and substitute fruit juice. These teetotaler cakes can last a long time if they are stored in airtight tins, but alcohol is the key ingredient of a true fruitcake.

Early versions of fruitcake were carried on long campaigns by Roman legions and the Crusaders. Sometimes, fruitcake that was made from a past year's harvest was shared to invoke blessings on the current year's harvest.

Delayed consumption is a fruitcake tradition. A fruitcake that is given as a gift is rarely eaten right away. Indeed, "regifting" is a fruitcake ritual, and some of the most legendary fruitcake creations last for decades.

Q: Why did Abraham Lincoln have an air corps?

A: On June 18, 1861, Abraham Lincoln received an extraordinary message. "I have the pleasure of sending you this first telegram ever dispatched from an aerial station," his correspondent wrote, noting that from his vantage point, he could see the countryside surrounding Washington, D.C., for fifty miles in any direction. The "station" was an enormous hot-air balloon that was tethered across from the White House and hovering five hundred feet in the air. Thaddeus Lowe, the balloon's operator, had run a telegraph line from the passenger basket down to a ground cable that was connected to both the president and the Union Army War Office.

A self-taught scientist, engineer, and aeronaut, Lowe had been piloting balloons for a decade. He was also an ardent supporter of the Union. He had mounted his balloon demonstration because he wanted to serve his country—not on the ground, like other soldiers, but in the air. One of the Union's greatest fears was that the Confederacy would launch a sneak attack on Washington, D.C., via northern Virginia. Who better to keep an eye on enemy maneuvers, Lowe asked, than a spy in the sky?

Lincoln agreed. A few days later, on June 21, he created the Union Army Balloon Corps and appointed Lowe as its chief. Over the next two years, Lowe made three thousand balloon ascents. His telegraph apparatus relayed crucial information to the ground troops. During the Peninsula Campaign of 1861–62, Lowe alerted General George McClellan to the movements of rebel troops three miles away; it was the first time in history that a commander was able to use aerial intelligence to route an enemy. At the Battle of Fair Oaks (May 31–June 1, 1862), Lowe's messages guided an entrapped Union battalion to safety.

Ever alert for new possibilities, Lowe also commandeered a barge from which he could make balloon ascents over the Potomac River, thus creating the first "aircraft carrier." His constant presence in the sky was such an irritant to the South that he became, according to author Carl Sandburg, "the most shot-at man of the Civil War." Though his balloon sailed too high for Confederate artillery to reach—the craft could climb to five thousand feet— Lowe did have a few close calls. At one point, he actually caught a cannonball in his basket.

Despite his daring, Lowe's balloon corps proved too controversial for the army. Rival balloonists, perhaps jealous of his success, accused him of mismanaging funds. Some generals found the balloons too cumbersome and expensive to transport. In addition, Lowe himself suffered ill health from a bout of malaria. The corps was officially disbanded in August 1863, and a disappointed Lowe returned to civilian life.

His exploits were not forgotten, however. He received the Franklin Institute's Grand Medal of Honor in 1886. A mountain near Pasadena, California, bears his name. And in 1988, he was posthumously inducted into the U.S. Military Intelligence Corps Hall of Fame, the sole balloonist among its honorees. It is a fitting tribute to the nation's original spy in the sky.

Q: Why are there stripes on bowling pins?

A: As any modern-day hipster can tell you, bowling is more about fashion than rolling a ball into a rack of pins. So perhaps it's not surprising that even bowling pins pay homage to the style gods. With a pair of sweet stripes like an ascot around its neck, a bowling pin resembles a 1950s Frenchman on a yacht trip off the Riviera.

Okay, so maybe bowling pins aren't inspired by haute couture. (But don't try to tell us those shoes aren't!) Actually, bowling pins are a classic case of form following function. It's been a long evolution: Archaeologists have found evidence of bowling pins dating back almost two thousand years.

Those first bowling pins were made of stone, but by the late nineteenth century, bowling-pin manufacturers had turned to maple as their material of choice. These early pins were made from a solid block of wood, but problems with splintering and uneven weights led to inconsistent pin behavior and lower scores than bowling's governing body at the time, the American Bowling Congress (ABC), liked to see.

Pin manufacturers eventually discovered that gluing pieces of maple wood together and coating them with a synthetic lacquer not only made it easier to produce pins with more consistent weights, but also resulted in a sturdier pin. Pins are still generally made from maple, despite experiments with steel, plastic, and even magnesium.

Nowadays, all bowling pins are standardized according to specifications set by the United States Bowling Congress (or USBC, as the former ABC is now known). These specifications include height and weight measurements, as well as the circumference of different parts of the pin. Nowhere in the specs, however, is there a mention of stripes, though the USBC does allow for pins to have "neck markings."

So why stripes? According to representatives of both the USBC and Brunswick Bowling, there is no particular reason. The striping convention first appeared early in the twentieth century, as bowling's popularity grew and companies began mass-producing bowling equipment. These stripes were nothing more than a form of decoration—a stylistic flourish.

Stripes aren't the only bits of flair to appear on pin necks. For example, Brunswick manufactures some pins with crowns around the necks. We, however, are partial to the image of ten Frenchmen in ascots. It's way more fashionable.

Q Why do crows always take the most direct route?

A Those large, perching black birds are pretty darn smart, maybe even smarter than your toddler. Can your kid count aloud up to seven, say more than one hundred words, and speak in complete sentences? Well, some highly intelligent crows can—they mimic the human voice, much like a parrot does.

Now, as for being smart enough to know the most direct route, perhaps you're thinking of the expression "as the crow flies." That means traveling in a straight line, or taking the fastest or shortest route from point A to point B. Some think this idiom is based on the notion that crows, being very shrewd, always fly straight to the nearest food supply.

Ornithologists will tell you that some crows—such as the American Crow—do indeed fly with very deliberate, flapping wing beats. However, if you take a look out the window, you might notice your neighborhood crows aren't necessarily flying on the straight and narrow. In fact, in their forage for food, they're probably swirling around in patterns similar to large, wheeling arcs.

So what gives? Well, "as the crow flies" is actually a very old expression. The earliest known printed use of the phrase came in 1767, when William Kenrick wrote this in *The London Review of English and Foreign Literature:* "The Spaniaad [sic], if on foot, always travels as the crow flies, which the openness and dryness of the country permits; neither rivers nor the steepest mountains stop his course, he swims over the one and scales the other."

Need a translation? Kenrick alludes to the fact that crows (and apparently Spaniards) are not encumbered by obstacles of land, road, or sea. For humans, though, rivers, mountains, and construction detours on U.S. Route 20 often force us to take deviating and more time-consuming paths.

Case in point: The distance between Key West, Florida, and Pensacola, Florida, is 524 miles directly across the Gulf of Mexico, as the crow flies. But if you MapQuest that trip to drive by car, you'll be riding all the way up the Sunshine State for about fourteen hours, or a distance of about 808 miles.

So it seems the idea that crows always take the most direct route has more to do with colloquial phraseology than literal fact. Truth is, any flying bird is able to get between two points without being hindered by roadblocks. But that doesn't mean you should sell those crafty crows short.

It turns out these birdies were quite the feathered friends to early sailors. According to the U.S. Navy's *Origin of Navy Terminology*, crows were once carried onto ships as a sort of onboard GPS system. In cases of poor visibility, a crow was released into the air.

Why? Crows are landlubbers, so they inevitably headed straight toward dry land. This allowed the navigator of the ship to plot a course to shore, even in foggy weather. Now just where were these fowl crewmembers kept? In a cage, high up on the ship's main mast: the "crow's nest," of course!

Q Why does it cost more to insure a red car?

A Red, the color of blood and fire, is considered to be energizing and passionate. Crimson cars, then, are known to attract all kinds of trouble, including drivers who like to push the pedal to the metal. Think the cops don't know it? A gray car and a red car are exceeding the posted speed limit. Which one is the trooper going to pull over? Thought so.

It gets worse. Speeding correlates to high-risk behavior, a factor in traffic accidents. Insurance companies track moving violations. Do you think flinty actuaries who calculate auto premiums charge more for red cars in anticipation of high collision claims? Actually, think again. When it comes to car insurance, much of what we believe about red is wrong.

Insurance companies are well aware of the red rumor. It was the number-one myth that was identified in an online survey of one thousand drivers conducted in 2005 by DriveSM, a Progressive Group auto insurance company. Of the drivers surveyed, 25 percent believed that car color affects auto insurance rates.

This notion makes underwriters see red. They assert that car color is not used to calculate auto insurance rates; instead, premiums are based on the vehicle's year, make, model, body style, and engine type. In general, the newer and more expensive the vehicle, the costlier it is to repair and, therefore, to insure. The youngest and oldest drivers pay more because they have the highest accident rates. The same holds true for men versus women, singles versus married people, and urbanites versus country folk. Miles driven plays a role, and so does your driving record, including, yes, moving violations.

If drivers of red cars do indeed behave in inordinately risky ways, America's multibillion-dollar insurance industry would probably know it. A spokesperson for State Farm Insurance, the nation's largest auto insurer with policies on forty million vehicles, notes that the legions of actuaries are highly motivated to predict risk. If they could set higher rates for red cars, they would.

Q Why are salaries a taboo topic?

A Everybody, it seems, wants to tell all. Don't believe us? Just turn on the TV news; most nights you'll see people whose lives have recently been rocked by personal tragedy but who nonetheless have time to pour their hearts out to anybody brandishing a camera, a microphone, and an expensive haircut. At the bookstore, you'll find stacks of magazines and memoirs that are filled with stories related by famous and not-so-famous people who want to tell us way more about themselves than we need to know—who they slept with, what they snorted. The Internet is teeming with blogs in which people from all walks of life tell us the mundane details of their existences.

But getting people to talk about their salaries? Well, that's not so easy.

According to Ed Lawler, a business professor at the University of Southern California, talking about how much money you earn can make you appear uncouth. "It's a very American, very middle-class phenomenon," Lawler told *The New York Times*. "The way we were raised is that it was bad taste to talk about how much you make." Lawler, who studies salary secrecy, says that many people see no constructive purpose in revealing their salaries. Why? Depending on how much money the other people in the conversation earn, the information can make the blabbermouth look like a braggart or a loser.

Who really stands to gain from this secrecy? Lawler and others who study the issue agree: employers. Knowledge is power. The less we know about how much our coworkers are getting paid, the easier it is for employers to keep our salaries down. This is one reason why some companies reprimand their employees for discussing their compensation. Lawler has conducted multiple studies that have found that people tend to overestimate how much their coworkers get paid. They assume that their lower salaries are the exception and that most other people get paid more. If they only knew.

But it appears that more and more that younger people do know. A study conducted in 2007 for *Money* magazine discovered that people under the age of thirty-five are more willing to discuss their salaries with coworkers. Having grown up as the Internet was exploding onto the scene, they seem more comfortable than their elders with the dissemination of any and all personal information. The ease of Internet anonymity has given rise to a slew of sites where people report their occupations and the wages they earn, allowing others to compile ballpark salary figures for job hunters to use.

The same people who enjoy embarrassing themselves on Twitter and Facebook also have fewer qualms about the traditional social constraints with regard to talking about money. And in the long run, that may pay off for them.

Q Why can't we remember much of anything that happened to us before the age of three?

A To spare us the horrific memories of constantly soiling our diapers? Laugh if you will, but Sigmund Freud actually offered an explanation along these lines. Freud, ever the ray of sunshine, believed that we repress our earliest memories because they're uniformly traumatic. (What exactly did this guy's parents do to him?)

Of course, subsequent scientists have had little use for Freud—they've forwarded their own theories. One post-Freud analysis suggested that young children lack the internal equipment to form long-term memories; the prefrontal cortex and hippocampus—the memory centers of the brain—aren't yet developed enough.

Later studies have demonstrated that it's not that simple. Small children actually *do* have the ability to form lasting memories. A 1994 study, for example, found that 63 percent of twenty-three-month-olds could recall events that they experienced at eleven months. (These tiny tots couldn't talk, of course, so the experiment was designed to teach them a unique series of actions and then see if they could still perform them a year later.) This study, and others like it, show that we have the ability to form long-term memories before we can even talk.

In fact, talking is where the trouble begins. According to some studies, the memory starts working differently once language kicks in. Scientists in New Zealand conducted an experiment to observe memory formation in children who were just learning to talk. When the subjects were two or three years old, with limited language skills, they were exposed to a memorable stimulus: a machine that appeared to shrink big toys into smaller toys. (Don't get excited—it was just an illusion.)

The researchers followed up with the kids later, when their language abilities had further developed. While many of them remembered the mysterious machine, they could only describe it using words and actions that were in their repertoire at the time of their exposure to it. Even though they had developed a greater vocabulary that would have allowed them to describe the magical machine with more clarity, they didn't use these words.

This suggests that our early memories become inaccessible because of a change in the way we think. Before we can talk, our worlds—and our memories—are based solely on disconnected impressions of images and sound. As we learn to talk, we develop the ability to tell stories and the ability to structure our impressions into cohesive plots that become narrative, or "autobiographical," memories. While we're learning to talk, we have access to our pre-language memories, but we can't translate them to fit with our new way of thinking. Pre-verbal memories aren't reinforced by and connected to the narrative memories, so they gradually disappear into thin air.

The lesson? Don't bother dropping thousands of dollars on the big Disney World trip before your kid can talk and can remember it.

Q Why do zebras have stripes?

A The zebra is among the flashy few of the animal world. Like the butterfly, the tiger, and the peacock, the zebra looks like it treated itself to a vanity paint job. Which is why one of the theories explaining the evolutionary advantage of those flamboyant stripes sounds counterintuitive: The stripes may actually help zebras blend in.

For one thing, vertical stripes can mesh pretty well with the vertical lines made by the tall grass that covers the ground in much of the zebra's natural habitat. There's a noticeable color difference, of course—tall grass comes in shades of yellow, green, and brown that don't exactly match the zebra's stark black-and-white coat. But this probably doesn't matter much, since the zebra's primary predators—the lion and hyena—seem to be colorblind.

The stripes may also provide the zebras with another way to visually confuse their predators. Zebras usually stick together in herds, where the clusters of vertical stripes can make it tricky for predators to figure out where one zebra ends and the other zebra begins. A lion, for example, might have difficulty homing in on any specific zebra, especially the more vulnerable foals. And once the herd starts to move, it's just a blur of stripes.

Some zoologists don't put much stock in the camouflage theory and suggest that the real evolutionary advantage of stripes has to do with a zebra's social life. Every zebra has a unique stripe pattern that can allow the animal to easily identify a friend (or perhaps a mortal enemy). Each zebra's stripe pattern serves as a sort of name tag, a way to be identified within a massive herd. Stripes may also help zebras stick together when predators attack, even at night. In case of emergency, zebra logic may say, follow the stripes.

Another theory suggests that zebra stripes are really a type of bug repellent. Tsetse flies, like other parasitic biting arthropods, seem to be drawn to large, one-colored surfaces—after all, that's how most large animals can be identified. But zebra stripes defy the norm, which may cause the tsetse flies to overlook the beasts when they're hunting for a free meal. There's strong evidence to support this theory: First, tsetse flies bite zebras much less frequently than they do other big animals. Second, there are more tsetse flies in the regions of Africa where zebras sport more pronounced patterns of stripes.

Of course, it's possible that the stripes may serve all of these purposes, at least to some degree. Or perhaps zebras are simply showing off.

Q: Why are ineligible college athletes called redshirts?

A: Ask *Star Trek* fans what a "redshirt" is, and they'll tell you that it's a term that's used to describe a stock character who is introduced into a storyline, only to be killed by the end of the episode. Ask Italians what a "redshirt" is, and they'll point to a portrait of Giuseppe Garibaldi as they hum a few bars of Italy's national anthem. Ask college football fans what a "redshirt" is, and they'll stare at you blankly for a few minutes before asking you to pass the chips.

This is not so much a reflection of the IQ of the average football fan as it is of the general confusion surrounding the term "redshirt." Part of the problem is this: Although the term is bandied about quite often in discussions of college sports, "redshirt" isn't an official term of the governing body of college athletics, the National Collegiate Athletic Association (NCAA). Furthermore, try as you might, you won't find any college athletes sitting on the sidelines actually wearing red shirts—unless red is the color of their uniform, of course.

Much of the confusion is rooted in the NCAA's rules of eligibility for college athletes. Essentially, all college athletes are given, upon initial enrollment, five years to complete four years of competition. Because of this rule, some college athletes skip a season of play in order to extend their eligibility. In order to earn a fifth year of eligibility, the player must not participate in any sanctioned competition during the skipped season. Not one play in a football game, not one pitch in a baseball game—any participation whatsoever uses up one year of eligibility. There are hundreds of detailed rules that further define eligibility; in fact, many college athletic departments have entire divisions devoted to merely interpreting and applying the rules for their own players.

College athletes might choose to sit out a season for a number of reasons, including injury, academic issues, or because the player isn't physically and/or mentally ready to play at the college level. These athletes are allowed to practice with the team, essentially making the skipped season an extended training session. When this practice first started in college sports, these athletes would wear red shirts during practice to differentiate them from eligible players—hence the term "redshirts." The word entered the lexicon in September 1950, according to the *Oxford English Dictionary*, when it was used in a Birmingham, Alabama, newspaper article.

Nowadays, red-shirting is a common practice. College sports are a multibillion-dollar industry, and the players are auditioning for multimillion-dollar jobs in the professional ranks. So the next time you're watching the big game at a buddy's house and the announcer refers to a player as a redshirt freshman, you can enlighten your friends about the term and its origin. Just make sure to pass the chips first.

Q Why is it good to be a wise man but not a wise guy?

A To be sure, there's a stark contrast here—the former is a smart person, the latter is a smart aleck. The sayings of a wise man should be ignored at one's own peril, while the sayings of a wise guy should be ignored, period. But taken at face value, shouldn't the two refer to the same thing (that thing, of course, being a person of great wisdom)? Well, that's the funny thing about colloquial English: Appearances are often deceiving.

When reference is made to a wise man, it's safe to say that everyone within hearing distance is on the same page. A wise man is one who is savvy to the ways of the world. This dates to Biblical times, when three wise men (also referred to as the Magi) followed a star to the birthplace of Jesus. They were called "wise men" because they practiced astrology and divination and were thought to have supernatural knowledge. (The origin of the word "Magi"—*Magus*—is the same as the origin of the word "magician.")

The wise guy, as we have come to know him, is a much younger specimen. His origins are harder to pin down. The term "wise guy," meant ironically, was part of the American vernacular by the end of the nineteenth century. It is most likely a derivation of the term "wiseacre," which has the same meaning: Both refer to one who puts up a pretense of knowledge, especially in a specific area, to mask one's own ignorance.

Wiseacre most likely is derived from the Middle Dutch word *wijssegger*—pronounced *wai-zegger*. *Wijssegger* refers to a soothsayer or a prophet; in English, it has always been used ironically. This twisted translation appeared in English for the first time in 1595, in a popular ballad.

The reason for this ironic translation is most likely due to age-old enmity between the English and the Dutch. There are many phrases in the English language in which Dutch people are referred to in a derogatory manner: "Dutch courage" is the courage one acquires through alcohol consumption; a "Dutch nightingale" is a frog; and a "Dutch concert" is a particularly offensive cacophony. Quoting the Dutch word for wise man, but meaning the opposite, is probably just a jab at Dutch intelligence.

Though the origins are murky, the difference is clear: Heed the message of the wise man; disregard that of the wise guy. And take what the English say about the Dutch with a grain of salt.

Q Why would anyone buy an aluminum Christmas tree?

A For the same reason anyone bought cars with fins or transistor radios: The aluminum tree was once the latest high-tech, shiny, groovy gadget.

On a cold and gray Chicago morning in December 1958, Tom Gannon saw a unique, homemade metal tree in a Christmas display at a Ben Franklin five-and-dime discount store. The favorably impressed Gannon was the toy sales manager of the Aluminum Specialty Company of Manitowoc, Wisconsin—and by the following Christmas, his firm had the aluminum Christmas tree on the market. It was a hit. Over the next ten years, Aluminum Specialty Company sold more than one million Evergleam trees in sizes ranging from two to eight feet tall. At least forty other companies jumped on the bandwagon, and aluminum trees were manufactured through the 1970s.

The trees were modern and flashy. Their metallic sheen complemented any color scheme, and ornaments glittered off the sparkling boughs. They also were reusable—individual branches fit into holes in the trunk, so that when the holidays were over, the whole bundle of holiday cheer could be carefully taken apart and shoved in the attic until next Christmas. There was just one downside: The electrical conductivity of the branches made strands of Christmas lights a no-no. But some owners used rotating floodlights to bathe their trees in different tints as a substitute for that tradition.

So who killed the aluminum Christmas tree? One unlikely suspect is a certain prematurely bald youngster from the funny pages. In 1965, CBS premiered *A Charlie Brown Christmas*. The animated film used a big pink aluminum tree as a symbol of yuletide commercialism and fakery. Was it coincidence that the popularity of aluminum trees took a nosedive soon after? Whatever the cause, suddenly you couldn't give aluminum trees away. Tastes changed, and everyone wanted a natural, sweet-smelling, green Christmas tree. Even fake trees went green.

Today the vintage aluminum models are sought-after collectibles, and nostalgic reproductions of aluminum trees go in and out of fashion. Like fins on cars, aluminum trees evoke a specific era. Those who remember such trees from their childhoods look at them fondly—for about five minutes. Then they wonder, "What was I thinking?"

Q Why do bees die after they sting?

A You're out in the yard on summer day, pulling weeds in the garden, flipping burgers on the grill, or lounging in the shade. Suddenly, you feel the sharp tip of a bee's stinger in your skin. What did you possibly do to deserve it? Sure, it's just a bee sting, but it hurts!

While you are still smarting from this unprovoked attack and are cursing all of the insects on the planet, you can take consolation in the notion that the bee might have given up its life when it recklessly chose to sting you. We really should explain that, shouldn't we?

First, it depends on the type of bee that stung you. Only honeybees die after stinging. The honeybee has a large barb on its stinger; when the bee stings, the barb usually catches in the victim's skin. (This only happens when a honeybee stings a victim possessing elastic-like skin that can entangle the barb, like a human. If the barb doesn't get caught, the honeybee can fly off to sting another day.)

As the stuck honeybee tries to dislodge its stinger, it usually tears its abdomen, along with muscles and nerves, causing the insect to die within a few minutes. If you think about it, this is kind of a horrific way to go.

The honeybees that sting are always females and are known as worker bees. The queen bee is the only sexually mature female in a colony and the only one capable of laying eggs. Instead of having an ovipositor (egg-laying organ) like the queen, a worker has a barb. When a worker bee perceives a threat to itself or to the hive, it stings.

A typical hive has thousands and thousands of workers, so a few lost on occasion hardly matters. You might say that it's a job to die for.

Q: Why do your ears pop in an airplane?

A: Frequent air travelers know they can rely on a few things during each flight. One, a minibag of pretzels and a plastic cup of warm Sprite will be the poor excuse for an in-flight meal. Two, the in-flight entertainment will be a Jim Carrey movie, most likely *Ace Ventura II*. And three, twenty minutes before landing, the infant who has been sleeping peacefully in the row behind you will wake up and begin shrieking nonstop until you land. Is *Ace Ventura II* that bad? Well, yes, it is. But that's probably not why the child is shrieking. More likely, it's because of excruciating ear pain.

Right behind your eardrum is something called the middle ear, a little air-filled space that helps in the transmission of acoustic waves. The air pressure in the middle ear is imperative to your tympanic health—too much pressure and the eardrum could burst; too little and it could collapse. Usually, that air pressure is stable because of how air pressure works in the environment. As we remember from physics class (okay, as we nerds remember from physics class), air pressure changes with altitude—the higher you get, the lower the pressure.

Whenever air pressure changes, the air pressure in the middle ear also must change to reach equilibrium with the external air pressure. When you're rising—such as during takeoff—the pressure in your middle ear is greater than the pressure outside, and air needs to escape. The escape hatch is known as the Eustachian tube, which connects the middle ear to the throat. During takeoff, this pressure calibration is pretty easy for your ear to achieve on its own. (Think of how easy it is for an inflated balloon to release air.)

However, landing is another story. As a plane descends, the pressure outside becomes greater than the pressure in your middle ear. Left untended, that pressure difference can create a vacuum that makes for a painful earache. Fortunately, we grown-ups know how to force open the Eustachian tube, allowing air to rush into the middle ear and equal the pressure. This can be accomplished by swallowing, chewing gum, blowing your nose, or yawning. The popping you hear during takeoff and landing is the sound of the air rushing in or out of your middle ear.

This also explains why babies tend to shriek on airplanes. Because infants are not capable of willfully forcing open their Eustachian tubes, they suffer as the air pressure outside begins to change. One solution is to give the baby a pacifier or bottle—the sucking motion can help unblock the Eustachian tube and relieve the pain. If this doesn't work, try turning off the in-flight entertainment.

Q Why does time seem to move faster as you get older?

A Many of the "benefits" of growing old seem to involve decreased speed. It takes longer to walk across the room because we're not as fleet of foot. We speak more slowly as our aged brains struggle to keep pace with our mouths. Amorous advances require a little more patience because of certain physiological transformations. And then there's the driving-slow-in-the-left-lane deal.

But nature appears to quicken one thing as we age: the passage of time. The older we get, the more often we find ourselves saying,

"Really? That happened twelve years ago? I thought it was more like three years ago."

In 1975, University of Cincinnati professor Robert Lemlich published a paper on time perception. (We could swear it was more like 1988.) Working on the assumption that as a person ages, each year accounts for a smaller fraction of his or her entire life, Lemlich devised an equation comparing one year in the life of a forty-year-old to one year in the life of a ten-year-old. He concluded that time goes by twice as fast for the forty-year-old. To arrive at this finding, he divided ten years into forty, took the square root of that result, and ended up with the number two.

Understand? We don't, either. We just thought it necessary to include some science in the answer. But it's Lemlich's basic premise that's important: The longer you live, the shorter any given increment of time seems relative to the length of your life. Time isn't moving faster, but your perception of time changes.

Proof? When you're five, a year of kindergarten seems like an eternity. But when you're fifty, that annual prostate exam seems to come up about every six weeks.

Q Why is a marathon 26.2 miles?

A To most of us, running a marathon is incomprehensible. Driving 26.2 miles is perhaps a possibility, though only if we stop at least once for Fritos. Equally incomprehensible is the number itself, 26.2. Why isn't a marathon 26.4 miles? Or 25.9?

Why Are There More Women Than Men? • 55

For the answer, we must examine the history of the marathon. Our current marathon is descended from a legend about the most famous runner in ancient Greece, a soldier named Philippides (his name was later corrupted in text to Pheidippides). For much of the fifth century BC, the Greeks were at odds with the neighboring Persian Empire; in 490 BC, the mighty Persians, led by Darius I, attacked the Greeks at the city of Marathon. Despite being badly outnumbered, the Greeks managed to fend off the Persian troops (and ended Darius's attempts at conquering Greece).

After the victory, the legend holds, Philippides ran in full armor from Marathon to Athens—about twenty-five miles—to announce the good news. After several hours of running through the rugged Greek countryside, he arrived at the gates of Athens crying, "Rejoice, we conquer!" as Athenians rejoiced. Philippides then fell over dead. Despite a great deal of debate about the accuracy of this story, the legend still held such sway in the Greek popular mind that when the modern Olympic Games were revived in Athens in 1896, a long-distance running event known as a "marathon" was instituted.

How did the official marathon distance get to be 26.2 miles if the journey of Philippides was about twenty-five? In the first two Olympic Games, the "Philippides distance" was indeed used. But things changed in 1908, when the Olympic Games were held in London. The British Olympic committee determined that the marathon route would start at Windsor Castle and end in front of the royal box in front of London's newly built Olympic Stadium, a distance that happened to measure 26 miles, 385 yards.

There was no good reason for the whims of British lords to become the standard, but 26.2 somehow got ingrained in the sporting psyche. By the 1924 Olympics in Paris, this arbitrary distance had become the standard for all marathons.

Today, winning a marathon—heck, even completing one—is considered a premier athletic accomplishment. In cities such as Boston, New York, and Chicago, thousands of professionals and amateurs turn out to participate. Of course, wiser people remember what happened to Philippides when he foolishly tried to run such a long distance. Pass the Fritos.

Q Why was smallpox so deadly for Indians, but not Europeans?

A The Europeans were not good guests in the New World. Whether it was conquistadores in the Caribbean, Pilgrims in New England, sailors in Fiji, or settlers in Australia, they left a calling card no one wanted: diseases that killed thousands of people. Some experts think that smallpox and other diseases, such as measles and influenza, killed up to 95 percent of the native populations of these locales—in other words, only one in twenty people survived.

Yet the Europeans remained ridiculously healthy. And when they sailed back home, they brought no new illnesses with them. Why?

The Europeans had already been exposed to epidemic diseases—or at least their ancestors had. Smallpox was known in ancient Egypt, and a smallpox epidemic killed millions of Romans in the second century AD. The disease hit Europe so frequently that the folks who had no natural immunities died off. Those who lived passed their immunities on to their children. Over the centuries, with so many nasty plagues hitting big population centers, the surviving Europeans became more resistant to the killer microbes.

Where did these diseases originate? Was there a Patient Zero? No. Most of the epidemic bugs—smallpox, measles, influenza, and even tuberculosis—came from livestock. When Asians and Europeans began herding cattle and penning up ducks and pigs thousands of years ago, they breathed in the strange germs that hung around the animals. Once humans started living in cities in large numbers, these germs were able to spread like wildfires. Europe suffered through the same plagues that killed so many Indians and islanders, but Europe's experience took place hundreds of years earlier, and its populations recovered.

The conquistadores, Pilgrims, sailors, and settlers who crossed the seas during the Age of Exploration came from families that had survived waves and waves of disease. Without realizing it, they brought smallpox, measles, and influenza germs with them to infect people who had never seen cattle, never herded animals, and never, ever been exposed to any of these diseases.

You know the result: Millions died. Exactly how many millions is unknown because experts aren't sure about the sizes of pre-encounter populations. The first wave of smallpox to hit Mexico's Aztec Empire in 1520 killed half the kingdom. Up to ten million perished, including the emperor. More disease followed, and a century later, the area's native population numbered only 1.6 million.

Here's another infamous example: In 1837, smallpox hit the Mandan, an Indian tribe in North Dakota. The disease, brought by someone who was on a steamboat traveling up the Missouri River, almost destroyed the tribe. Within weeks, the Mandan population of one village dropped from two thousand to forty.

And since no one back then knew about germs, microbes, or how sicknesses spread, the Europeans weren't even aware of what they'd done.

Q: Why does the color red anger bulls?

A: Red has been the color of choice of bullfighters for centuries. Their bright red capes are used to incite their bovine opponents into spectacular rages. In fact, the phrase "seeing red" is believed to have originated from the fury that the color seems to provoke in the bull. What is it about red that ticks off bulls?

The truth is: nothing. Bulls are partially color-blind and don't respond to the color red at all. The red color of the cape is just eye candy for the audience, much like the bullfighter's *traje de luces* ("suit of lights").

Then is it the motion of the cape that infuriates the bull? The truth is: no. There's nothing that the matador does that makes the bull angry—it's in ill humor before it even enters the ring. These bulls aren't bred to take quiet walks in the park on Sunday afternoons. No, they are selected because they exhibit violent and aggressive behavior. By the time they hit the bullfighting arena, just about anything will set them off.

We're talking about bulls that have personalities that resemble John McEnroe's. The color red doesn't make them angry—*everything* makes them angry. Then again, the bullfighter plunging his sword into the bull's neck might have something to do with the beast's nasty disposition, too.

Q Why don't Grape-Nuts contain grapes or nuts?

A In a 1992 *Saturday Night Live* sketch, Jerry Seinfeld played the host of a quiz show for comedians. Seinfeld poked fun at his own penchant for riffing on the banalities of daily life by posing some questions, including, "What's the deal with airplane food?" and "What is the deal with Count Chocula?" and "Grape-Nuts—you open it up, no grapes, no nuts! What's the deal?" The "contestants" were stumped; apparently, so were *SNL*'s writers, because no good answer to the Grape-Nuts query was presented.

To be fair, this is a question that surely has been asked quite often since 1897, when C. W. Post invented the grain-heavy breakfast food. Essentially a shredded brick of baked wheat and malted barley, Grape-Nuts cereal has nothing remotely resembling grapes or nuts on its ingredient list—and it never has.

For most of us, breakfast cereal is about as inseparable from an American childhood as Saturday morning cartoons—but it wasn't always that way. Until the late nineteenth century, a typical American breakfast consisted of eggs, bacon, and sausage. Heart disease was rampant, though its causes were poorly understood and treatments were virtually unknown. Those who escaped cardiovascular disease ran the risk of developing gastrointestinal disorders because of the near-absence of fiber in the typical American diet.

This began to change in 1863, when Dr. James Caleb Jackson—head of a Dansville, New York, sanitarium—concocted a fiber-rich bran nugget that he hoped would bring relief to the troubled bowels of his patients. Unfortunately, these nuggets required overnight soaking merely to be chewable. Even more unfortunately, Jackson opted to call his breakfast item Granula, a name that evokes a blood-sucking grandmother, not a healthy meal.

Americans were not impressed. But the idea stuck around, and a couple of decades later, another doctor, John Harvey Kellogg—if the last name sounds familiar, it should—created his own version of a fiber-rich breakfast item. Never much of a wordsmith, Kellogg also named his creation Granula; he ultimately changed it to Granola after a trademark dispute with Jackson.

One of Dr. Kellogg's patients was C. W. Post. Confident that he, too, could make an edible breakfast food, Post set out to create his own whole-grain cereal made of baked wheat and barley. Not being much of a scientist, Post believed that the sucrose that formed during his cereal's baking process was grape sugar. Nor did Post have much of a palate: He thought that his creation tasted nutty. Hence, Post named his new breakfast cereal Grape-Nuts.

Though Post might have been somewhat disconnected from reality, he was a clever marketer. By the turn of the twentieth century the nation had developed a taste for breakfast cereal, and Post positioned Grape-Nuts as a healthy option. Americans bought both the marketing claims and the cereal—Grape-Nuts has become one of history's best-selling breakfast foods even though it has no grapes, no nuts, and no flavor.

Q: Why are there only two sexes?

A: Aren't dating and marriage complicated enough as it is? Imagine having to contend with dozens of genders. We'd never stop yelling at each other. But if you put relationship difficulties aside, it seems like it would make better sense to have a plethora of sexes—or maybe even just one.

Biologically speaking, the top priority in life is to reproduce. In a species with only two sexes, you can mate with only 50 percent of the population, assuming the sexes are distributed equally. If you added a third sex, you could mate with two-thirds of the population. If there were ninety-nine different sexes, you could mate with 99 percent of population. And in a species with only one sex, you could mate with 100 percent of the population. From this point of view, two is actually the worst possible number of sexes for finding a mate. Why, then, do almost all animal species comprise two sexes?

According to the leading scientific theories, human beings and other animals are divided into two sexes because of specialized biological machines called "mitochondria." These microscopic power plants exist inside all of your cells, converting the chemical energy stored in the food that you eat into a form of energy that your body can use. Without mitochondria, life as we know it could not exist.

Mitochondria share many of their features with primitive bacteria—in fact, scientists now suggest that our mitochondria actually evolved *from* bacteria, millions and millions of years ago. The prevailing theory is that, in the far-off mists of time, a single-celled organism engulfed a bacterium, probably in an attempt to eat it.

But instead, the two worked out a symbiotic relationship—the organism gave food to the bacterium, which, in turn, produced a vast amount of energy that the organism could use to sustain a higher level of development.

Even though our mitochondria seem to have once been an independent form of life, they are now firmly integrated as components of our cells. But there's still a genetic holdover from their bacterial origin. Normally when we think of DNA, we picture the genetic information inscribed on the chromosomes inside the nuclei of our cells—the genetic material that determines our hair and skin and eye colors, shapes our personalities, and controls the creation of almost every component of our cells. Every component, that is, except those mysterious mitochondria. That's because each mitochondrion has its own internal DNA (called mitochondrial DNA or mtDNA), stored on a simple loop. It's more like the primitive DNA of bacteria than the complex chromosomes in the nucleus of a cell.

Another major difference between your mitochondrial DNA and your normal DNA is that you inherit your mtDNA entirely from your mother (and from her mother, and from her mother's mother, and so on). This has led scientists to theorize that there's a serious evolutionary advantage—although they don't agree on what exactly it is—if only one parent's mtDNA is passed on to the couple's offspring. According to this theory, the biological differences between the two sexes first emerged as a way to ensure that only one parent in a couple could give mtDNA to the next generation.

In early organisms, the differences between the two sexes—let's call them passers and non-passers—were slight. But over millions and millions of years of evolution, the organisms became incredibly more complex and each of the two sexes grew increasingly distinct. Eventually, the passers became female and the non-passers were male.

There are a few species with multiple versions of males—not quite a third sex, but close. For example, certain species of harvester ant have one type of male with sperm that produces worker ants and another type that is designed to make queen ants. At any rate, the basic two-sex system works fine for most species.

Q: Why is Thanksgiving on Thursday?

A: Because Abraham Lincoln said so. It's almost as simple as that. In his 1863 proclamation, Lincoln declared Thanksgiving to be an official national holiday. It was one way he attempted to unite the nation in the midst of the brutal Civil War. Here's what he said: "I do therefore invite my fellow citizens in every part of the United States, and also those who are at sea and those who are sojourning in foreign lands, to set apart and observe the last Thursday of November next, as a day of Thanksgiving and Praise to our beneficent Father who dwelleth in the Heavens."

Thanksgiving was celebrated long before Honest Abe came along and gave a speech about it. According to American tradition, the Pilgrims' first Thanksgiving was observed in 1621 (it probably took place in mid-October, and no one knows for sure on which day of the week). Although the Pilgrims did not celebrate Thanksgiving the following year, over time it became a tradition for days of thanksgiving to be celebrated throughout the colonies following the fall harvest. But not all the colonies honored Thanksgiving, and not all observed it on the same day.

A unified Thanksgiving Day came about largely due to the efforts of Sarah Josepha Hale. As editor of the popular magazine *Godey's Lady's Book*, Hale campaigned for a single, national day of thanksgiving for a number of years—until Lincoln granted his support in 1863. That year, Thanksgiving was celebrated on Thursday, November 26.

Why Thursday? Well, it was good enough for George Washington, who declared a one-time national day of thanksgiving on a Thursday in late November 1789. In addition, according to *The Old Farmer's Almanac*, Thursday might have become a traditional day of thanksgiving for the Puritans in order to distance the commemoration from the Sabbath day.

In 1939, President Franklin Roosevelt announced that Thanksgiving would be celebrated on the third Thursday of November instead of the last. This was an attempt to encourage earlier holiday shopping and boost the economy during the Great Depression. But not all the states complied until Congress passed a resolution in 1941 declaring that Thanksgiving would fall on the fourth Thursday of November, and that's where it remains today. Kind of makes you crave a piece of pumpkin pie, huh?

Q: Why is America called America?

A: Weren't you paying attention in your eighth-grade world history class? As you were undoubtedly told, the Americas are named for the Italian explorer Amerigo Vespucci. But what did he do that was so great? The only fact about his life that anyone seems to remember is that, well, America is named after him. How did a dude who's otherwise forgotten by history manage to stamp his name on two entire continents?

While he didn't make the lasting impression of his contemporary Christopher Columbus, Vespucci was no slouch. As a young man, he went to work for the Medici family of Florence, Italy. The Medicis were powerbrokers who wielded great influence in politics (they ran the city), religion (some were elected to be bishops and popes), and art (they were the most prominent patrons of the Renaissance, commissioning some of the era's most memorable paintings, frescos, and statues).

Like many of the movers and shakers of that age, the Medici had an interest in exploration, which is where Vespucci came in. Under their patronage, he began fitting out ships in Seville, where he worked on the fleet for Columbus's second voyage. Vespucci evidently caught the exploration bug while hanging around the port—between 1497 and 1504 he made as many as four voyages to the South America coast, serving as a navigator for Spain and later Portugal. On a trek he made for Portugal in 1501, Vespucci realized that he wasn't visiting Asia, as Columbus believed, but a brand-spankin' new continent. This "ah-ha" moment was his chief accomplishment, though he also made an extremely close calculation of Earth's circumference (he was only fifty miles off).

Vespucci's skills as a storyteller are what really put his name on the map. During his explorer days, Vespucci sent a series of letters about his adventures to the Medici family and others. Vespucci livened up ho-hum navigational details with salacious accounts of native life, including bodice-ripping tales of the natives' sexual escapades. Needless to say, the dirty letters were published and proved to be exceedingly popular. These accounts introduced the term "The New World" to the popular lexicon.

German cartographer Martin Waldseemüller was a fan, so he decided to label the new land "America" on a 1507 map. He explained his decision thusly: "I do not see what right any one would have to object to calling this part after Americus, who discovered it and who is a man of intelligence, [and so to name it] *Amerige*, that is, the Land of Americus, or *America*: since both Europa and Asia got their names from women."

But there are those who believe that Vespucci's forename wasn't the true origin of the name. Some historians contend that the term "America" was already in use at the time and that Waldseemüller incorrectly assumed it referred to Vespucci. Some have suggested that European explorers picked up the name Amerrique—"Land of the Wind" in Mayan—from South American natives. Others say it came from a British customs officer named Richard Ameryk, who sponsored John Cabot's voyage to Newfoundland in 1497 and possibly some pre-Columbian explorations of the continent. Yet another theory claims that early Norse explorers called the mysterious new land *Ommerike*, meaning "farthest outland."

In any case, the name ended up on Waldseemüller's map in honor of Vespucci. The map proved to be highly influential; other cartographers began to use "America," and before long it had stuck.

Keep this story in mind the next time you're composing a heart-stoppingly boring e-mail—if you spruce it up a bit, you might get a third of the world named after you.

Q Why do doctors have such lousy handwriting?

A An estimated seven thousand Americans die each year due to incorrect medication or dosages brought about by doctors' sloppy handwriting on prescriptions. Why can't well-educated, literate, responsible, confident medical professionals write legibly? Because doctors are likely to be men—and men in executive positions have lousy handwriting. That's according to a study posted on bmj.com, an online medical journal. It turns out that doctors' handwriting is no worse than that of their peers in other important professions.

Why are doctors singled out? Because what they write—it can be a life-saving prescription—is in a sense powerful and magical. So are doctors themselves, with their special knowledge and exalted position. In this context, their chicken scratches seem oddly infantile and out-of-sync with their training and standing. It's made worse, experts agree, by the arcane symbols that doctors have long used to indicate dosages and schedules, and now by the huge array of drugs with similar-looking names that are easily confused on a sloppily written prescription.

There has been a movement for years to implement prescription-writing computer software that transmits letter-perfect scrips to pharmacies. But this has been slow in coming. Critics argue that it's just as easy to choose the wrong drug on a drop-down menu as it is to write "Celebrex" so illegibly that a busy pharmacist sees "Cialis," and some poor dude's arthritis doesn't get better at all.

Here's some sound advice: Look at your prescription and ask your doctor to repeat it to you. Then make sure your pharmacist understands it the same way. If there's a discrepancy, alert your pharmacist to call your doctor. Your life may depend on it.

Q Why doesn't water in a water tower freeze?

A Although our chemistry teacher more likely compared us to Linus Van Pelt than Linus Pauling, even we know that water freezes at thirty-two degrees Fahrenheit. Which is why we've never understood why water doesn't freeze in water towers during those long, cold winters.

To fully understand why you're able to turn on your faucet and have running water even on the coldest days, we need to look at how water towers work. Most towns get their water from wells or bodies of water such as lakes. This water is pumped to a water treatment plant, where it is disinfected before being delivered through a main pipeline to the rest of the area's delivery system. A water tower is hooked up to that system, drawing water into its reservoir as it is pumped through the main pipes. When the demand for water is too much for the system pump to handle, gravity and water pressure release water from the tower back into the main pipeline. During off-peak times, the water tower refills from the pipeline.

This is a simple, efficient system, and one that helps explain why water towers don't freeze solid in the winter. When a water tower pulls water from the pipeline to refill its reservoir, it is drawing somewhat warmer water from the pipes. Furthermore, water towers are drained and refilled fairly frequently, making it difficult for ice to form. The agitation of water molecules from the movement of draining and refilling slows down the freezing process, too. (To get an idea of the way this works, think of how long it takes waterfalls or rivers to freeze.)

However, in some parts of the country—such as the frozen tundra of North Dakota—water in water towers does freeze. Rarely, though, does it freeze solid. In climates where freezing is a danger, water towers are more heavily insulated, and some are even built with heating systems near their bases that prevent water from freezing on its way into the tower.

Of course, no precautions are foolproof. Just about anything can freeze over if it's cold enough for long enough: lakes, waterfalls, water towers, and, if our passing grade in high school chemistry is any indication, even hell.

Q Why do onions make you cry?

A American poet Carl Sandburg once said: "Life is like an onion: You peel it off one layer at a time, and sometimes you weep." If chopping a Vidalia always has you reaching for the tissue box, there may be some comfort—or rather, discomfort—in understanding why.

For starters, the pungent odor and flavor of the onion come primarily from the natural sulfuric compounds it contains. When you peel and slice through one of these odoriferous bulbs, the sulfuric compounds escape into the air in the form of a volatile gas. And when this volatile gas reacts with the moisture in your eyes, well, that's when the burning, stinging waterworks ensue.

Sulfuric acid is the corrosive substance used to make fertilizer, explosives, rust remover, and drain openers—and it's what's created in the unfortunate chemical exchange between onion and eye. Even though it's a very mild form of sulfuric acid, the nerve endings in your eyes are highly sensitive to the irritation.

To dilute the acid and protect your eyes, your brain sends a signal to your tear ducts to produce more water. This is the point at which you'll likely rub away the tears with your onion-juiced hands and make it much worse. (Don't do this next time!)

Instead, try a tear-reducing trick. The National Onion Association says that one effective solution is to chill an onion for thirty minutes before slicing. Then cut off the top and peel the outer layers, leaving the root end intact. The cells that release the sulfuric compounds are concentrated at the base of the onion, so cutting off the root end last should help lessen the sting.

If you can multitask, try holding a wooden spoon, a sugar cube, a slice of lemon, or a piece of bread between your teeth as you chop. Some "onionologists" say that these items will absorb the gas before it reaches your eyes. But for those of you who want to circumvent this pesky issue altogether, go to your local store and pick up pre-chopped onions. You'll find them in the produce or freezer aisle.

Q: Why do professors wear blazers with elbow patches?

A: Just as soldiers are clad in fatigues and New York Yankees players wear pinstripes, the brave souls who enter the cutthroat arena of academia don the vestments of their own venerable field. For college professors all over the world, this means, of course, a blazer with elbow patches. As ubiquitous among them as the petty need to undermine the achievements of their colleagues, the jacket with patched elbows has become the standard (if unofficial) uniform for academics. But where did this fashion statement come from in the first place? God knows, people can't wear these things because they look cool.

According to noted fashion writer Bruce Boyer, the impetus to reinforce the elbow of a tweed jacket with a leather patch was born purely of necessity. As it happens, college teachers in the United Kingdom would routinely receive ye olde shaft when it came to their salaries; some educators earned little more than room and board. Professors struggling to make ends meet would naturally try to wring an extra season or two out of their already disheveled attire by patching up any wear and tear. The elbows were the first area of the jacket to wear thin—no doubt from long hours spent leaning over a lectern while pontificating on the world's weighty issues—but leather patches were also often applied to the cuffs, lapels, and button holes.

This professorial parsimony seems sensible enough—we can all understand the impulse to save a few bucks here and there. But it still doesn't explain why brand new jackets are sold with the leather elbow patches already in place. Perhaps this is just a genteel instance of our apparent appetite for pre-distressed clothing. One can enter any mall in America and purchase jeans that have been designed to look well worn even when new—not just "broken in," but completely mangled with carefully placed rips and tears. We're really all just cattle waiting for the next fashion trend to sweep through the high-density feedlot.

Q Why do the Dallas Cowboys and Detroit Lions always play on Thanksgiving?

A You could call it a tradition that's as American as apple pie, except that it happens on the one day of the year that apple is trumped by a different flavor of pie. Despite the fact that few people have any interest in ever seeing the Detroit Lions play, and because most people love to hate the Dallas Cowboys (no Thanksgiving feast is complete without at least a dash of animosity), millions of Americans look forward to that one special Thursday in November when they can do what they usually get to do only on Sundays: eat too much and watch a lot of professional football. The games are as much a part of Thanksgiving as turkey and stuffing.

But the truth is, Americans used to get a lot more football on Thanksgiving than they do now. As many as six games were played on a single Thanksgiving during the 1920s; of course, television was not yet even a glint in the nation's eye, so hardly anyone saw them. Just as the holiday football tradition began to wane, the Chicago Bears rolled into Detroit for a 1934 Thanksgiving showdown. The Bears were the defending NFL champions and had an 11–0 record; the Lions were 10–1.

The Western Division championship was on the line, but the Lions were new to Detroit that year and attendance had lagged—the largest crowd of the season had been about fifteen thousand. So it's not surprising that Lions owner George A. "Dick" Richards took notice when twenty-six thousand people showed up on Thanksgiving for a game that was broadcast nationally on NBC radio. Richards made sure the Lions played host to the Bears on Thanksgiving for the next four years, and a national event was born.

The tradition took a hiatus during World War II, but the Lions picked it up again in 1945, and they have played on every Thanksgiving since. During the 1950s, when football and television began their torrid romance, the Lions were in their heyday and had nationwide appeal. They hosted the Green Bay Packers every Thanksgiving from 1951 to 1963. It was usually the only game of the day, until the upstart American Football League began staging its own Turkey Day matchup in 1960.

In 1966, the NFL decided to counter by boosting its holiday offering to two games, and Cowboys president and general manager Tex Schramm was quick to seize the opportunity. "I was very aware of the impact of television," Schramm said. "What does everybody do after they eat turkey? They sit and watch TV." As the Lions descended into mediocrity, Dallas became known as "America's Team."

But traditions die hard, so the Lions continue to serve up our national appetizer each Thanksgiving. Shortly thereafter, the Cowboys deliver the main course. (There have been two exceptions to this rule: The St. Louis Cardinals replaced the Cowboys as hosts in 1975 and 1977.)

The tradition has, in fact, evolved somewhat. In 2006, the NFL added a night game that is intended to function as our national dessert—for those hardy souls who manage to remain conscious into the evening.

Q: Why does Australia have so many poisonous snakes?

A: Many people associate the cute and cuddly koala with Australia. And that's exactly the image the nation's tourism industry wants to tout: cute and cuddly. Deadly and dangerous wouldn't sell as many vacation packages, though it would be more accurate.

Australia is a place that would drive the snake-phobic Indiana Jones to the brink of insanity—there are snakes, snakes, and more snakes, many of which are poisonous. Of the approximately six hundred known venomous snakes in the world, a whopping sixty-one reside in Australia, according to the University of Sydney. And the Australia Venom Research Unit reports that eight of the ten most toxic land snakes on the planet are native to the continent.

Cute and cuddly? We think not. Thirty-five percent of the snake species in Australia are poisonous. Why does this continent host so many scary slitherers? Hundreds of millions of years ago, Australia was part of the supercontinent Gondwana, which also included South America, Africa, India, New Zealand, and Antarctica. Gondwana began to break up one hundred and fifty million years ago, and Australia snapped off altogether about fifty million years ago.

The snakes that were on the terrain now known as Australia included those from the Elapidae family, a group that had many venomous varieties. Once this land mass became surrounded by water, the snakes had nowhere to go. So they developed ways to survive on this biodiverse continent, which has a rain forest, vast deserts, and the largest coral reef on the planet. As is the case with natural selection, the strongest varieties lasted; many of today's venomous serpents are descendents of the Gondwana castaways.

Australia's venomous snakes come in a variety of lengths and colors, and they reside in many of the continent's environments. The deadliest—not just on Australia, but on the entire planet—is the inland taipan. This snake, part of the ancient Elapidae family, has venom potent enough to kill one hundred humans in a single bite. Close behind on the venom chart are the eastern brown snake and mainland tiger snake, which also hail from the dreaded Elapidae clan. Both can seriously ruin a vacation.

But don't let these snakes—or the continent's other poisonous critters, such as the box jellyfish or the funnel web spider—scare you away. If you visit Australia, the main predator you'll need to beware of is the human—specifically, those who are driving cars. Auto accidents cause more deaths each year in Australia than all of its poisonous creatures combined.

 Why are vitamins good for us?

 Put it this way: How would you feel if your skin broke out in huge bruises, your gums became so soft that your teeth fell out, your old cuts started to bleed again, and—to top it off—the broken leg that healed several years ago suddenly snapped in two?

Awful? Sure. Scurvy is an awful disease. It's caused by lack of vitamin C. Fortunately, vitamin C is found in a wide range of fruits and vegetables. For more than a hundred years, British sailors were called "limeys" because they drank rations of lime juice to ward off scurvy on long voyages.

No one knew why lime juice worked until 1911, when Casimir Funk, a Polish-American chemist, isolated a substance in food he dubbed a "vital-amine." *Vital*, after the Latin word for life, and amine because he thought the substance was an ammonia-based compound. Later, it was discovered that vitamins were not genuine amines, but the name stuck.

So what are vitamins? Unlike calories, we do not burn them for energy, nor are they used to build muscle mass, like proteins. Yet vitamins help us metabolize food and construct cells. Many are coenzymes that bind with enzymes and act as catalysts for biological functions. In other words, a coenzyme is like the team captain who makes sure the coach's orders reach each player throughout the game.

There are two kinds of vitamins: water-soluble and fat-soluble. Water-soluble vitamins—which include vitamin C, all the B vitamins, and folic acid—dissolve into the bloodstream, where they are carried directly to tissues and set to work. Vitamins A, D, and K are fat-soluble. They must be absorbed from the intestines by large fatty cells called lipids before they reach the bloodstream. Every vitamin has a unique purpose, but in general, water-soluble vitamins aid with metabolism while fat-soluble vitamins help keep cells strong. Water-soluble vitamins pass through the body quite rapidly; we need to replenish them often. Fat-soluble vitamins are stored in the liver for quite some time.

Vitamins are also known as micronutrients, which means that a little goes a long way. Although many people believe mega doses of vitamins make them healthier, there's no proof that this is so; in fact, too many fat-soluble vitamins can overload the liver, leading to serious illness.

Why do vitamin names jump from E to K? What happened to vitamins F, G, H, I, and J? Well, those vitamins are closely related to B and were eventually included in the B vitamin spectrum. However, vitamin research is being conducted all the time, and scientists are always discovering new micronutrients. You never know when another vitamin will show up.

So eat those fruits and veggies. Vitamins are good for you, from A to (maybe someday) Z.

Q Why do cats always land on their feet?

A It's true: Cats have an uncanny ability to survive a fall. Maybe that's why we say they have nine lives. However, the notion that they always land on their feet isn't exactly accurate. Every once in a while, a cat does indeed go splat. And it's probably because a very sorry owner left a window or balcony door open.

Cats are not afraid of heights. If they see a tasty bird or butterfly floating about outside, their predatory instincts kick in and it's jump time. This phenomenon is so common that a 1987 study of falling cats in the *Journal of the American Veterinary Medical Association* even gave it a name: High-Rise Syndrome. New York City veterinarians often use the term to describe the injuries that cats sustain after falling from the city's high-rise apartment windows.

Whether a cat lands on its feet after a fall depends on several factors, including the distance it plummets and the surface on which it lands. If a cat falls a short distance (say, fewer than one or two stories), it usually can right itself in midair. How? For starters, cats have an amazing sense of balance and coordination. Each of their inner ears is outfitted with a vestibular apparatus, a tiny fluid-filled organ that helps them register which way is up. When the cat is falling, the fluid in the inner ear shifts, telling the cat to reorient its head until the fluid is once again equalized and level.

When a cat turns its head and forefeet, the rest of its body naturally follows. How so? Cats have super-flexible musculoskeletal systems. A cat's backbone is like a universal joint—it has thirty vertebrae (five more than a human) and no collarbone. This is why cats are so agile. With this freedom of movement, a cat can instantly bend and rotate like a pretzel to land on its feet.

If a cat falls from more than one or two stories, it likely will sustain severe or fatal injuries, even if it can right itself. Its legs and feet simply cannot absorb all the shock. That said, the study in the *Journal of the American Veterinary Medical Association* revealed something really surprising: Of the 132 high-rise cats that veterinarians examined, those that fell from above seven stories had a better chance of escaping injury.

It seems that after plummeting five stories or so, cats reach a nonfatal terminal falling velocity. At this point, they are able to relax their muscles and spread their bodies out like feline parachutes or flying squirrels, and they arch their backs just before hitting bottom, reducing the force of the impact.

Just how far can a cat fall without being killed? The longest non-fatal fall on record is forty-two floors.

Q Why is IBM referred to as Big Blue?

A From its inception in 1911 as the Computing-Tabulating-Recording Company, International Business Machines Corp. has been perhaps the most powerful and sophisticated force behind society's obsession with the collection and storage of data. It would seem simple, then, to find out how IBM got its nickname, Big Blue. Surely somewhere inside this behemoth of a corporation, someone must have recorded the origins of the company's nickname and stored it in some special database for all eternity. Nope.

Even though IBM sometimes refers to itself as Big Blue and has incorporated "Blue" into the names of some of its products (Deep Blue, Blue Pacific, Blue Gene), the Armonk, New York-based firm can't definitively explain the source of its nickname. Of course, there are theories. Some sleuths believe that people started calling IBM Big Blue because the company's employees were required for many years to wear white shirts, which prompted a number of them to wear blue suits.

Perhaps a more cogent explanation is that IBM's logo has incorporated the color blue since the 1940s. The most plausible theory might be that the mainframes IBM sold in the 1960s had blue covers, which led sales reps and customers to coin the term Big Blue. Business writers picked up the term and popularized it.

As we move into our second century of high-tech data management, Microsoft has assumed the mantle that IBM once held as the king of business technology. Maybe someday it'll get a nickname. How about Not-So-Big Blue?

Q Why would anyone want to be the devil's advocate?

A Any plan that can't survive scrutiny deserves to fail, and it's the role of the devil's advocate to ferret out the flaws and shine a light on them. This isn't being needlessly argumentative. It's a hallowed responsibility—some might say that it's a sacred one.

Nonetheless, it can be a thankless job. When it comes to exposing foibles, there's a fine line between an honorable adversary and a horse's ass. But what's the devil got to do with it?

During the Renaissance, the Catholic Church needed a few good skeptics. In 1587, Pope Sixtus V created a judicial procedure for canonizing saints. Canonization required proof that the nominee had performed at least two miracles. One priest was chosen to present arguments against conferring sainthood—his task was to examine evidence thoroughly and note any sign that the miracles in question were not of a divine nature and could be explained by natural causes. To many Catholics, this was like taking Satan's side against faith and religious belief—it was like being the devil's advocate.

To its credit, the Vatican considered the role to be one of distinction and honor. The official title of the "devil's advocate" was *Promoter Fidei* ("Promoter of the Faith"). By challenging the faith, the advocate was actually strengthening it and, in the process, weeding out the less than saintly. One priest, Prospero Lambertini, worked as *Promoter Fidei* for twenty years; he then won a big promotion and ruled as Pope Benedict XIV from 1740 to 1758. Pope John Paul II eliminated the role of the devil's advocate in 1983. It was a controversial decision that left many Catholics wondering if the church had lowered the bar for sainthood.

The merits of a devil's advocate extend beyond religious matters, of course. Brazilian business consultant and mathematician Marcial Losada studies how groups make decisions, and he values the role of the devil's advocate. Losada notes, for example, that if no one at a marketing meeting likes a new product, but everyone goes along with it anyway in order to please the boss, the product is likely doomed. A new gizmo that is unanimously beloved is just as likely to fail, he says, if no one in the group steps up to scrutinize it for flaws before it goes to market.

Being a mathematician, Losada has reduced the dilemma to a formula called the "Losada Line." Basically, according to Losada's theory, every decision-making group needs a positive-to-negative ratio of almost three-to-one to succeed. In other words, for roughly every three yea-sayers, a business needs one naysayer as a reality check. So if you're a devil's advocate, stand up and be counted. Consider it your sacred duty.

Q: Why didn't the Vikings stay in North America?

A: Because they weren't particularly good guests, and the Native Americans threw them out. According to ancient Norse sagas that were written in the thirteenth century, Leif Eriksson was the first Viking to set foot in North America. After wintering at the place we now call Newfoundland in the year 1000, Leif went home. In 1004, his brother Thorvald led the next expedition, composed of thirty men, and met the natives for the first time. The Vikings attacked and killed eight of the nine native men they encountered. A greater force retaliated, and Thorvald was killed. His men then returned home.

Six years later, a larger expedition of Viking men, women, and livestock set up shop in North America. They lasted two years, according to the sagas. The Vikings traded with the locals initially, but they soon started fighting with them and were driven off. There may have been one further attempt at a Newfoundland settlement by Leif and Thorvald's sister, Freydis.

In 1960, Norse ruins of the appropriate age were found in L'Anse aux Meadows, Newfoundland, by Norwegian couple Helge and Anne Stine Ingstad. The Vikings had been there, all right. Excavations over the next seven years uncovered large houses and ironworks where nails and rivets were made, as well as woodworking areas. Also found were spindlewhorls, weights that were used when spinning thread; this implies that women were present, which suggests the settlement was more than a vacation camp.

The ruins don't reveal why the Vikings left, but they do confirm what the old sagas claimed: The Vikings were in North America.

The sagas say that the settlers fought with the local *Skraelings*, a Norse word meaning "natives," until the *Skraelings* came at them in large enough numbers to force the Vikings out.

This sounds plausible, given the reputation of the Vikings—they'd been raiding Europe for centuries—and the Eriksson family's history of violence. Erik the Red, the father of Leif, founded a Greenland colony because he'd been thrown out of Iceland for murder, and Erik's father had been expelled from Norway for the same reason. Would you want neighbors like them?

Q: Why do bruises turn different colors while they're healing?

A: If you take a lot of beatings, you've no doubt encountered a wondrous rainbow of bruising. Bruises aren't beautiful, but their weird mix of purple, blue, yellow, and even green can be oddly fascinating.

A bruise, or contusion, is an injury in which tiny blood vessels in body tissue are ruptured. As a small amount of blood seeps through the tissue to just below the skin, a deep red or purple bruise forms. The deeper within the tissue the vessels burst, the longer it takes for the blood to reach skin level, and the longer it takes for the bruise to form.

The body is an efficient machine—it's not about to waste the precious iron that's released from the blood when the vessels burst. It dispatches white blood cells to the scene to break down the hemoglobin so the body can salvage the iron.

This chemical breakdown has two notable by-products, each of which has a distinctive color: First, the process produces biliverdin, which is green; then it produces bilirubin, which is yellow. As the deep red hemoglobin, the green biliverdin, and the yellow bilirubin mix, a range of colors results in what we call a bruise. As the body heals, it gradually reabsorbs the by-products, and the skin returns to its normal color.

To minimize bruising, you can apply an ice pack several times a day for a couple of days after you're injured. Or you can invest in some karate classes.

Q: Why do doughnuts have holes?

A: The saga of how doughnuts came to have holes is a bit of a mystery; perhaps a police detective is needed to solve it. What cop wouldn't want to pore over mountains of evidence that involves doughnuts?

The origin of doughnuts most likely can be traced to Northern Europe during medieval times. Called *olykoeks* ("oily cakes"), the pastries came to America with the Pilgrims, who had picked up the recipe in Holland, their first refuge from England, which they abandoned for America in the early sixteen hundreds. The dough in the middle of these pastries rarely got cooked, so that area often was filled with apples, prunes, or raisins.

By the mid-eighteen hundreds, the pastries were being made with a hole in the middle—and this is where the plot thickens. Two stories about the origin of the hole involve Hanson Crockett Gregory, a sea captain from Rockport, Maine. One says that he poked out the middle of one of his wife's homemade doughnuts by plunging it into a spoke on the ship's wheel. That eliminated the uncooked middle, and it enabled Gregory to eat and keep his boat at an even keel at the same time.

A second story—this one slightly more plausible—involves Gregory eating doughnuts with other crew members. Tired of the raw dough in the middle, he took a tin off the ship's pepper box and used it to push out the middle, leaving only the cooked edges. He tasted it and exclaimed that it was the best doughnut he had ever eaten. Years later, in 1916, Gregory recounted this story in the *Washington Post*.

So, is Hanson Crockett Gregory the man we can thank for the doughnut hole? There is no real proof that backs up either account involving Gregory, but this much is certain: A plaque commemorating his culinary claim stands at the house in Maine where he lived. And perhaps not coincidentally, doughnuts did indeed have holes by the mid-eighteen hundreds, making them easier to cook and improving their taste.

Once they started coming with holes in them, doughnuts soared in popularity. During World War I, the French gave doughnuts to American soldiers to remind them of home. In the 1920s, doughnuts were the snack of choice in movie theaters. At the 1934 World's Fair in Chicago, they were called, "The food hit of the Century of Progress."

Such praise seems a bit extreme, although cops all over America would certainly agree.

Q: Why is Kansas City in Missouri and Missouri City in Texas?

A: In the vast expanse that is the United States, there are quite a few cities and towns that have the names of outside states. How about Virginia City, Nevada; Colorado City, Arizona; and Michigan City, Indiana? Pretty unimaginative—and confusing—huh?

In the case of Kansas City, Missouri, the town officially claimed the Kansas name before the state of Kansas existed. In 1838, John Calvin McCoy, who is regarded as the father of Kansas City, and thirteen other men bought 271 acres of land that was then known as the Gabriel Prudhomme farm. This property would become Kansas City's first downtown district, but first the men needed to agree on a name for their new township. According to legend, the owners considered several names, including Port Fonda, Rabbitville, and Possum Trot. In the end, they settled on Kansas, for the Kansa Indians who inhabited the area.

Kansas, Missouri, was chartered as a town on June 1, 1850, and as a city on February 22, 1853. In 1854, the Kansas-Nebraska Act established the boundaries of a large territory to the west, which was also given the name Kansas. The territory of Kansas became the thirty-fourth state in 1861. In 1889, the Missouri city known as Kansas officially changed its name to Kansas City to distinguish itself from Kansas the state.

As for how Missouri City came to be in Texas, that was a matter of marketing. In 1890, real-estate developers from Houston bought four acres of land near the BBB&C railroad. In an effort to draw settlers from the north to their new railroad, farming, and ranching town, the developers named the area Missouri City and launched an advertising campaign in St. Louis, Missouri.

Missouri City was touted as "a land of genial sunshine and eternal summer." Despite the developers' appeals to the residents of the Show-Me state, most of Missouri City's initial settlers came from Arlington, Texas. When a wave of settlers from the north did make it down to Missouri City the following year, they were greeted by a harsh blizzard that included twenty-eight inches of snow.

Q Why do drive-up ATMs have Braille?

A Ever since Helen Keller first met Anne Sullivan in the late eighteen hundreds, visually impaired people have made big strides in the United States. They can now easily use computers, read books, shop, and engage in a whole range of other activities that people associate with a normal life. Despite all of these advances, though, blind people still are unable to drive cars. Which leads to this question: Why is it necessary for drive-up automatic teller machines (ATMs) to have Braille pads?

There are a number of potential answers to this incongruous question. When one is dealing with sheer, unadulterated illogic, it is usually safe to look to the United States government first for a possible explanation. And sure enough, the government is behind the installation of Braille pads on drive-up ATMs.

In 1990, the government passed the American with Disabilities Act, a landmark bill that prohibits discrimination against disabled

Americans. One need go no further than Section 4.34 of the act, which specifically details that ATMs be outfitted with a special apparatus for people with visual impairments, to find the answer to our question. The act requires that all ATMs be accessible to the blind; it does not make a distinction between drive-up and walk-up automated tellers, and as a result, all ATMs are equipped with Braille pads.

Economists will point out that once the government deemed Braille to be necessary on ATMs, it was a matter of efficiency for ATM producers to put the pad on all ATMs, whether they be drive-up or walk-up. Producing both Braille and non-Braille ATMs would require different molds, different inventories, and other logistical inefficiencies. And since the presence of Braille dots doesn't hurt anyone, why not put them on every ATM?

Besides, the Braille on those drive-through ATMs might come in handy. One can imagine situations in which a visually impaired person would need to use a drive-up ATM—when riding in a cab, for example. (Would you give your PIN to a cab driver?) Of course, this doesn't explain how the blind are able to use an ATM touchscreen—but that's another answer to another question.

Q Why do Space Shuttle astronauts wear parachutes?

A NASA devised an escape system for Space Shuttle missions after the 1986 *Challenger* disaster, in which seven astronauts died when a rocket booster exploded shortly after liftoff. The parachutes that astronauts now wear are part of a coordinated plan that offers them a chance to bail out if problems arise during launch or landing.

For obvious reasons, jumping from the shuttle is impossible while its rockets are firing. But there are scenarios in which escape would be an option. One would be after the rockets finish firing but before the shuttle reaches space. Another would be if the rockets fail after launch and the astronauts face a dangerous emergency landing in the ocean.

How would an escape work? First, the crew would guide the shuttle to an altitude of about twenty-five thousand to thirty thousand feet—just lower than the altitude reached by commercial airline flights—and jump from the shuttle through a side hatch.

To avoid hitting a wing or an engine pod during their escape, the astronauts would extend a twelve-foot pole from the side of the shuttle, hook themselves to it, slide down, and jump from there. NASA's space suits are designed to work automatically during an escape. The parachute opens at fourteen thousand feet, and when the suit detects impact with water, the parachute detaches.

The astronauts have other gizmos up their sleeves (and pant legs) that help in an emergency. When water is detected, the suit automatically deploys a life preserver. Also contained within the suit is a life raft, complete with a bailing cup to remove water that sloshes into it. Once safely afloat, the astronaut can pull a set of flares from one leg pocket and an emergency radio from the other. The suit, which is designed to keep the astronaut alive for twenty-four hours, is pressurized, thermal, and even comes equipped with a supply of drinking water.

The explosion that killed the *Challenger* crew was sudden and caused instant death, so this escape system would not have helped them. But because of that tragedy, today's Space Shuttle astronauts are better prepared if they need to make a daring escape.

Q Why does a rattlesnake's tail rattle?

A People have ascribed many functions to the rattlesnake's rattle: attracting a mate, hypnotizing prey, calling other rattlers to arms. But because a rattler rarely rattles if the snake isn't startled or perturbed, the consensus seems to be that the main purpose of the feature is to warn nearby animals to keep their distances—all those except potential meals, that is.

The distinctive rattle was especially useful in the days of yore, when rattlesnakes were contending with thundering herds of massive, hoofed bison on the American plains. It was beneficial for all concerned: The snake avoided getting trampled, and the other guy avoided a venomous bite. A rattlesnake's rattle is made of keratin, the same hard stuff that's in fingernails and animal horns. Rattlesnakes are hatched with a "pre-button," a sort of starter rattle at the end of the tail. Soon, a larger keratin rattle segment, called a "button," grows at the end of the tail, beneath the skin. When the snake sheds its skin for the first time—about ten days after emerging from the egg—it sheds the pre-button, but not the button.

The button forms the first real rattle segment, while a new keratin segment starts forming at the end of the tail, behind the button.

When the snake sheds its skin again, the new segment pushes the button farther out, and another segment starts forming at the base of the tail. The process repeats itself each time the snake sheds its skin—typically, three to four times a year—and a new rattle segment is added. Basically, the tip of the tail is a segment-producing assembly line.

The segments grow in puzzle-piece shapes—this keeps them loosely attached. And this is why the rattle rattles: The segments have enough flexibility to click and clack together when the snake shakes its tail. To sound the alarm, the snake sticks its tail straight up and shakes it; the tail can move back and forth ninety times per second. The click-clack is so effective that some other varieties of snakes that have rattle-envy do lo-fi versions by rapidly shaking their tails in dried leaves.

These imitators obviously know that the rattle serves an important purpose. It's kind of like a sign that reads: KEEP MOVING, BUDDY, THERE'S NOTHING TO SEE HERE.

Q: Why do some people dream in black and white?

A: There's an old saying that nothing is less interesting than another person's dream—unless you are in it. Yet the mystery of dreams has fascinated philosophers and scientists for thousands of years. Aristotle wrote an entire treatise on the subject in 350 BC. Much later, around the dawn of the twentieth century, Sigmund Freud developed an elaborate system of dream interpretation that mostly involved sex.

For all the research that has been done on dream phenomena, surprisingly little has been learned about the function of dreaming. And outside of color symbolists and New Age dream interpreters, few researchers have worked in the area of colors in dreams. But according to studies conducted in the past several years, anywhere from 12 to 20 percent of people dream in black and white.

Several theories have been put forth to explain the drab dream worlds of those 12 to 20 percent. The first of these—corroborated by a number of different dream researchers, including Harvard's J. Allan Hobson, a pioneer on the subject—points to the ephemeral nature of dreams. Everyone has had the experience of waking up from a really cool dream, only to have the details of the plot fade away even as you are trying to confusedly relate them to your bored spouse or roommate at the breakfast table. In the same way, this research suggests, everyone dreams in color, but the memory of the colors fades as quickly as the details do. Most people forget their dreams as soon as they awaken or gradually over the course of a day. But this does not explain why a small percentage of the population reports dreaming in black and white.

Other researchers take a more Jungian tack, suggesting that colors, like the events and objects in dreams, are symbols of the subconscious. Different colors symbolize different emotions—red is passion and drive, blue is calmness and rest, etc.—and shades of gray symbolize a desire to shield oneself from subconscious messages. For example, a red truck in a dream might symbolize passionate assertiveness, while a gray truck might indicate a desire to mask that assertiveness.

Perhaps the most interesting theory about color in dreams was proposed by University of California-Berkeley psychologist Eric

Schwitzgebel in a 2002 paper, "Why Did We Think We Dreamed in Black and White?" Schwitzgebel looked at the history of dream research and noticed that the percentage of people who reported colored dreams began to plummet in the late nineteenth century, reached a low of about 30 percent in the late 1950s, and spiked back up as the twentieth century progressed.

Were people really that dull in the first half of the twentieth century? Perhaps. But Schwitzgebel points to something else: The popular forms of media during that period (photography, movies, television) were in black and white. Prior to the invention of photography, black-and-white coloring was rare. (Have you ever seen a classical painting in black and white?) But with the advent of black-and-white photography, many people thought of images—especially everyday images—as being in black and white.

With the rise of film and television, the phenomenon increased. Many of us think of our dreams as movies anyway, and it would be natural for people who had been exposed only to black-and-white film and photography to remember their dreams as drained of color. If Schwitzgebel's theory is indeed true, one wonders what the future trend might be. Perhaps everyone will start dreaming in CGI.

Q: Why is there a dropped-third-strike rule in baseball?

A: On the surface, baseball is pretty simple. In the memorable words of former major-league manager Lee Elia: "The name of the game is hit the ball, catch the ball, and get the [bleeping] job done." But getting the [bleeping] job done and maintaining that apparent simplicity requires a few rules for resolving unusual situations—for example, the infield fly and the balk—that most fans know about without ever fully understanding.

Such is the case with the dropped-third-strike rule (or, more accurately, the uncaught-third-strike rule). The philosophy behind the rule is based on common sense: A team in the field shouldn't be given credit for an out if it screws up at the end of the play. On a third strike, if the catcher drops the pitch, or if the pitch bounds away from the catcher, it's equivalent to any other fielder dropping a fly ball. The batter is free to try to reach first base, and the defense has to be more proactive to record the out, by either tagging the batter or throwing him out at first base.

Without some modifications, the dropped-third-strike rule would offer the defense an unfair advantage. This is where the rule gets a little confusing. Say there's a runner on first and no outs—on a third strike, the catcher could purposely drop the ball, obliging the batter to run to first, which would in turn oblige the runner on first to make a break for second. With the batter and runner caught off-guard, the catcher could pick up the ball and initiate an easy double play by throwing to second for the force-out, followed by a quick throw from second to first to retire the now-running batter.

To eliminate the possibility of this sort of chicanery, the dropped-third-strike rule only applies under the following conditions: when there are two outs and a double play is pointless, or when first base is open with fewer than two outs so there is no chance for a force-out. With fewer than two outs and first base occupied, the batter is out on strike three regardless of whether the catcher catches the pitch.

The infield fly rule is also designed to eliminate similarly cheap double (or triple) plays initiated by intentional errors with runners on base. Now, if you want to figure out the [bleeping] balk rule, you'll have to go to another [bleeping] article.

Q: Why do we have earwax?

A: What's that you say? Why do we wear slacks? If you are not hearing well, you may have a buildup of cerumen—the medical term for earwax—in your ears.

Earwax is produced in the outer ear canal, which is the tunnel between the externally visible part of the ear and the inner ear and is where the eardrum is found. The skin of the outer ear canal uses sweat glands to produce two types of ear wax: "dry" wax (which is gray and flakey) and "wet" wax (gooey and brown). Both are equally effective at their jobs—wet wax just has more lipids, or fatty substance.

So what exactly is the job of earwax? First, it keeps the skin of the ear moist; if we didn't have earwax, the dry skin inside the ear would be unbearably itchy. Second, it helps prevent infection; earwax has antibacterial qualities, and it keeps certain fungi from wreaking havoc on our ears. And third, earwax traps invaders such as dirt and dust, which might otherwise bust up the joint; think of earwax as the bouncer at the bar that is your inner ear.

As your ear produces new wax, the old wax is pushed out and is deposited onto your outer ear. The old wax either falls off or is rinsed off when you bathe. Doctors beg us not to stick cotton swabs, keys, knitting needles, or ice picks into our ears to clean them—the wax can take care of itself without our help. Sticking things into your ears is likely to push the cerumen deeper and compact it. You might even puncture your inner ear, which is an extremely painful experience that isn't recommended.

Some people produce excessive wax that needs to be removed; too much of the stuff can cause hearing problems and infection. Older people, in particular, tend to suffer from wax buildup, partly because of hair growth in their ears. If you are a candidate for wax removal, let the experts handle it—they'll coax out that burdensome wax using water, mineral oils, and/or syringes. These tools work a lot better, and are much less hazardous, than the pencil that's sitting on your desk.

Q: Why can Sherpas exist at higher altitudes than anyone else?

A: In the early twentieth century, when Westerners first began to dream of reaching the summit of Mount Everest, one lesson quickly became clear: It was fruitless to try to make the climb without a Sherpa.

For the average person, the atmosphere way up there—29,035 feet at the mountain's peak—is not all that different from being in outer space. The thin air and extreme cold make it a deadly environment. Hypoxia, also known as mountain sickness, sets in quickly, resulting in hallucinations and impaired judgment. (We'd argue that the mere decision to attempt such a climb might be ample evidence of impaired judgment.)

But Western mountaineers on those early expeditions noticed that their Sherpa guides often seemed impervious to the dangers of high altitude. They maintained their strength and breathed the thin air with ease. The cold didn't seem to bother them, either. All in all, they were downright cheerful, even under the most dreadful conditions. So Sherpas became indispensable climbing companions. Sir Edmund Hillary, a native of New Zealand, wasn't alone when he became the first person ever to reach the summit of Everest in 1953—Tenzing Norgay, his Sherpa guide, was right behind him, "taking photographs and eating mint cake," as Norgay later described it.

In 1963, after the first American expedition reached the summit, three climbers were unable to complete the descent of the mountain because of frostbite, and they had to be rescued by Sherpas. Teams of four Sherpas carried each man for two days. The climbers later reported that by the end of the first day, their Sherpa rescuers not only were unaffected, but they had even become competitive, racing each other back to base camp.

What makes Sherpas so special? The Sherpa people are a small ethnic group concentrated in the Himalayan regions of Nepal, India, and Tibet. About ten thousand of them live in the Khumbu Valley of Mount Everest at elevations of about ten to twelve thousand feet. The reasons for their resistance to the dangerous effects of high altitude remain a mystery. Some researchers believe that living in high-altitude villages for hundreds of years has created an inherent genetic predisposition in Sherpas that allows them to cope with the rarefied air.

Whatever the reason, the message is obvious: Always take a Sherpa with you on the way up Everest, and be sure to pack enough mint cake for everybody.

Q Why are objects in my car's side-view mirror closer than they appear?

A Because that's the way lawyers see things. Actually, the printed warning on the glass of your car's right-side mirror has more to do with optics than attorneys, though avoiding liability can never be ruled out where an automaker is concerned.

By noting that "objects in mirror are closer than they appear," designers are telling you the convex shape of the mirror has altered your perception of the distance between you and what's in the mirror. And since what's in the mirror might be a truck, and those of us who are about to change lanes might be fooled into thinking that said truck is farther away than it actually is, a warning is a fine idea.

What's happening is the image of the truck—or car or motorcycle—has been compressed so that the field of vision covered by the mirror can be expanded. The intent is to provide a more complete picture of what's in your over-the-right-shoulder blind spot. This is accomplished by making the right-side mirror slightly spherical in shape.

The advantage is that a wide-angle view takes in more than a flat mirror would. (Try looking into the back of a spoon for a demonstration.) The disadvantage is that when it comes to viewable objects, the mind associates smaller with farther away. Hence, the warning.

Incidentally, your car's left outside mirror is planar (flat) because it's closer to your eyes and merely moving your head a bit can expand its field of view. As in your car's planar inside rearview mirror, objects reflected appear near-natural in size.

Car designers have recently introduced aspheric side-view mirrors in which only a portion of the surface has pronounced convexity. Ford is pushing its Blind Spot Mirror, sort of a highly developed version of those little stick-on fish-eye mirrors available at auto parts stores.

A convex spotter blended into the top outer corner of the mirror provides a field of view optimized for each vehicle and is usable on left- and right-side mirrors. Already available on some higher-priced cars is a blind-spot warning system that electronically senses unseen objects to the side and alerts the driver with a beeping tone, a flashing light, or both.

Some car companies are even testing video camera systems that would do away with rearview mirrors altogether. Wonder what a lawyer who's had a cable TV signal go down will say about that?

Q Why are Persian rugs so expensive?

A If you think that Persian rugs are expensive because they can fly, brace yourself for some bad news: They have no magical qualities. But this doesn't mean they aren't valuable.

Persian is to rugs what Fabergé is to eggs: The term itself implies an expensive, well-crafted item. The Persian rug's reputation for being the best of the best goes back more than a thousand years.

Persian rugs are regarded as unique works of art, and because of the amount of knotting that's involved in creating them, they are extremely durable.

What does it take for a carpet to be a Persian rug? For starters, it has to come from Persia, which is otherwise known as Iran. (Iran was known as Persia to the Western world until 1935, when the country requested that it be called Iran. In 1959, it relented and said that either name was permissible. Today, Iranian artistry is called Persian, but the country, in a global political context, is referred to as Iran.)

Carpet weaving is an important aspect of Persian art and culture; it's estimated that weaving is the occupation of one of every seven Iranians. The rugs are made by hand, knot by knot, and are noted for their intricate and colorful designs. Persian adornments often have curved patterns, which are more difficult and time-consuming to create than geometric ones. It can take months or even years to finish a rug.

The value of a Persian rug depends on a variety of factors. The material that is used is one—luxurious silk is more expensive than cotton. In some designs, precious metals such as silver and gold are incorporated. The complexity of the knotting and the design also play a role. Some designs have up to a thousand knots per square inch. Age is important, too. You'll spend a lot more on a rug that's hundreds of years old than on one that's new.

Rugs from the Safavid Dynasty (1502–1736) represent the height of Persian quality. In June 2008, Christie's auction house sold a Persian rug from the Safavid Dynasty for $4.45 million. It doesn't fly, but it's still a great rug.

Q: Why do people shake hands?

A: In today's Western world, the handshake serves a number of purposes. It can be a greeting or a farewell, and it can signify congratulations or condolences. In business, a deal can be sealed with a handshake.

Where exactly did this quirky little custom originate? This question is the object of much debate, conjecture, and confusion, mainly because the handshake likely predates written history. Some historians trace the origin of the modern Western handshake—the clasping of hands—to medieval Europe. Back then, shaking hands was hardly a congenial gesture—it was more like a shakedown. Men would clasp hands to make sure that neither was concealing a weapon.

Eventually, the handshake matured into something more civilized. According to Philip A. Busterson's 1978 book *Social Rituals of the British*, writer and explorer Sir Walter Raleigh, who was noted for his manners, introduced the handshake that we know today in the late sixteenth century.

Since then, the handshake has become a nuanced custom. For instance, it's considered poor taste to greet someone with a handshake that's too strong; a limp handshake, on the other hand, is perceived as a sign of weakness. It is viewed as an insult to refuse a handshake or to fake a greeting by offering but not following through on a handshake.

Today, there are high-fives, low-fives, soul shakes, secret handshakes—you name it. The handshake's grip on civilization has tightened considerably since those days in medieval Europe, when some skin on skin meant, "I'm not going to kill you... at least not today."

Q Why isn't Scotland Yard in Scotland?

A British nomenclature is loaded with misleading terms. Plum pudding is not pudding, nor does it contain plums. Real tennis doesn't have much to do with real tennis. Spotted Dick is a delicious dessert. Given this legacy of verbal imprecision, it's perhaps not surprising that the headquarters of the famous police force that patrols London is called Scotland Yard.

It started in 1829, when Charles Rowan and Richard Mayne were charged with organizing a citywide crime-fighting force. At the time the two men lived together in a house at 4 Whitehall Place, and they ran their fledgling outfit out of their garage, using the back courtyard as a makeshift police station. "Rowan and Mayne's Backyard" wasn't an appropriate name for the headquarters of a police force.

Instead, it was called Scotland Yard. Why? London police don't play bagpipes; haggis isn't part of the rations; and as far as we know, London policemen don't wear kilts (at least not in public). So what gives?

You might think that a mystery like this would be a perfect case for Scotland Yard. Unfortunately, those famed investigators aren't sure how their hallowed institution got its name, which is not necessarily a compelling endorsement of their detective work. After years of research, though, word detectives have narrowed the origin of the name to two likely possibilities.

According to the first explanation, Scotland Yard sits on the location of what was once the property of Scottish royalty. The story goes that back before Scotland and England unified in 1707, the present-day Scotland Yard was a residence used by Scottish kings and ambassadors when they visited London on diplomatic sojourns. The other, less regal possibility is that 4 Whitehall Place backed onto a courtyard called Great Scotland Yard, named for the medieval landowner—Scott—who owned the property.

Regardless of the name's true origin, the Metropolitan police have moved on—sort of. In 1890 they decided that they needed new digs and moved to a larger building on the Victoria Embankment. Given a chance to redeem themselves and give their headquarters a name that actually made sense, what did the London police choose? New Scotland Yard.

Q Why do traffic lights use the colors red, yellow, and green?

A This is reminiscent of a question you might find on a driver's education test in high school: "What do the colors of a traffic light indicate?" The answer: "Red equals stop, green equals go, and yellow equals slam on the gas." But why red, yellow, and green? Why not purple, pink, and blue? What does it matter, anyway?

For the answer, we need to look at the history of traffic signals. The first traffic light was for pedestrians, not vehicles. In 1868, outside the British House of Parliament, a railroad employee named J. P. Knight installed a gas-powered two-light signal. Being a railroad man, J. P. borrowed the signaling pattern used for train traffic: Red meant stop, and green meant proceed with caution. Unfortunately, the machinery was somewhat limited, as it had to be operated by hand. It also had a tendency to explode, which it did rather dramatically barely three weeks after being put into operation, killing the constable manning it.

It was more than four decades before traffic lights were given another shot, in the USA. With the Ford Motor Company putting a car in every driveway, the nation's roads were becoming a free-for-all. In 1914, tired of watching maniacs driving recklessly through Cleveland streets, the city fathers had an electric traffic light installed on Euclid Avenue, a street we can assume everyone started avoiding. This light used the same red-green system as the exploding British traffic signal; it wasn't until 1920 that a Detroit policeman thought of putting a yellow light between the red and green to indicate the lights were changing.

Why did that original pedestrian signal have red and green to symbolize stop and go? The colors were already the norm in the electrical industry, but how that choice was made in the first place is lost to history. Some color theorists surmise that red is traditionally associated with danger (think blood and fire), while green is linked to pleasing emotions (think spring).

However, these very same theorists claim that yellow denotes health and happiness. Funny—we would have thought haste and hurry.

Q Why do you get "brain freeze" from eating or drinking something cold?

A We're all familiar with "brain freeze," the searing head pain that occurs after a rapid ingestion of cold liquid or food. It's the body's way of saying, "Slow down. You don't have to finish that entire gallon of ice cream in two spoonfuls." What miracle of evolution produced such an effective safety measure?

There aren't a lot of concrete answers—scientists aren't even sure what causes a normal headache—but here's what we know: The headache associated with brain freeze lasts about thirty to sixty seconds and can occur in just about any region of the cranium (front, sides, back, top). Brain freeze is clinically known as a "referred" pain because while the stimulus is in the mouth or throat, the pain manifests itself in what a layman might describe as the brain. Brain freeze is much more likely to occur in hot weather than cold, and it usually peaks after about ten seconds.

Finally, brain freezes are not fatal. Why is this last bit important? You see, gentle reader, researchers spend the bulk of their time getting to the bottom of medical issues like cancer and heart disease, so a detailed analysis of cold-stimulus headaches will just have to wait until those other mysteries are solved.

Nevertheless, there is no shortage of theories about brain freeze. The prevailing one is that brain freeze is caused by vascular changes. "Vascular" is just a fancy way of describing the systems that ship fluids such as blood around your body. The coldness of, say, ice cream overstimulates the trigeminal nerve—which carries sensory information from the face, teeth, and tongue to the brain—causing the arteries that lead to the brain to contract.

This means there is less oxygen-rich blood flowing to your head. To compensate, the blood vessels in the brain expand to let more blood through. The expansion and contraction of these blood vessels is what many researchers believe causes headaches such as brain freeze.

Brain freeze certainly serves the purpose the body intends. Few of us can continue gorging on ice cream while experiencing its wrath. If only the body had similar defenses for other poor choices—maybe an uncontrollable sneezing fit before you buy a Michael Bolton album.

Q Why does the Leaning Tower of Pisa lean?

A To understand why the tower leans, one should know the history of this remarkable crooked edifice, including where it was built. At the turn of the first century AD, Pisa was a vibrant seaport city on the northwestern coast of Italy. In 1063, the Pisans attacked the city of Palermo. (And yes, this is where the phrase "Hey, Pisan!" comes from.) They were victorious and returned home with treasures.

The Pisans, being a proud people, wanted to show the world how important their city was, and decided to erect a great cathedral complex, called the Field of Miracles; the complex included a cathedral, cemetery, baptistery, and bell tower.

Pisa was originally named Poseidonia in 600 BC, from a Greek word meaning "marshy land." Bonanno Pisano, the original architect of the bell tower, did not think this was important information when he began the project. In 1173, Bonanno decided that since there was a good deal of water under the ground, he'd build a shallow foundation, one that was about three meters deep.

Five years later, when third-floor construction was about to begin, Bonanno realized that his structure was sinking on one side; this was because he built upon a bed of dense clay. But being a proud Pisan, he continued to go skyward. To attempt to solve the problem, he added two inches to the southern columns and thought no one would notice. People noticed. The third floor reached completion, and the job was halted indefinitely.

In 1272, construction of the bell tower resumed under the guidance of architect Giovanni di Simone. He completed four more floors, built at an angle to compensate for the listing. But not only did his remedy cause the tower to tilt in the other direction, but it also created a curve. In 1284, the job was once again halted. In 1319, the Pisans picked up their tools and completed the seventh floor. The bell tower was added in 1372, and then it was left to lean in peace until the nineteenth century.

In 1838, the foundation was dug out so visitors could see how it was built, which caused the tower to lean even more. Then in 1934, Benito Mussolini ordered the foundation to be reinforced with concrete. The concrete was too heavy, however, and it sunk the tower further into the clay.

Since then, many projects have come and gone; the tower is now stabilized and was reopened in 2001, so tourists can walk to the top. The Leaning Tower of Pisa is the top tourist attraction in Tuscany. The circular tower stands nearly 185 feet tall, is estimated to weigh almost sixteen thousand tons, has a 294-step spiral staircase, and leans at an angle of almost four degrees, meaning that the tower is about four meters off vertical. And to top it off, researchers from the University of Pisa found the tower to be sinking at a rate of one-twentieth of an inch annually. At that rate, they've predicted, the tower will collapse in fewer than three hundred years.

Q: Why aren't people covered in hair like other primates?

A: Life would be much more confusing at the zoo, for one thing. Cover us in fur and the line between ape and man gets a lot blurrier.

Scientists have proposed a few explanations for why people are mostly hairless. In the 1970s, the hot theory was that early humans entered a semi-aquatic phase—they spent their days catching fish and eating plant life in shallow waters. Like whales and hippos, humans lost their fur in favor of a layer of fat under the skin, which is a better insulator in the water.

But there are some holes in this theory—the most notable being that hanging out in African lakes and rivers is dangerous, thanks to crocodiles and nasty water-born parasites. If we had spent that much time in the water, critics say, we would have developed better defenses against the parasitic worms and such that still kill people in Africa today.

Speaking of parasites, a more recent theory speculates that we lost our fur as a defense against lice, fleas, and the like. When you're covered in fur, parasites are a major problem—but the insulating benefits of a flea-ridden coat of fur make the problem worth enduring. Until you've invented clothing, that is. As soon as humans could make their own clothes and build their own shelters, fur became a liability.

The problem with this theory is that the timing doesn't work—scientists have traced our fur loss back about 1.7 million years, yet evidence of clothing goes back only about forty thousand years. Still, even if parasite avoidance wasn't the driving force in our loss of fur, it might help to explain why we think smooth, hairless skin is sexy today. Think back to our caveman days, and you'll see why we might have been hardwired to favor hairlessness. If you had no body hair, a potential mate could clearly see whether you had parasites; if you didn't, it suggested that you were healthy and would produce strong offspring.

But back to how we lost our fur in the first place. The most popular theory nowadays is that the scorching savannah was just too darn hot. As humans gradually developed a new foraging and hunting lifestyle, they began leaving the cool jungles behind for long treks in the hot sun.

And then, just as now, humans cooled off by sweating. As our hirsute ancestors chased their prey across the vast savannahs, they would have soaked their furry coats in no time, making it even more likely that their bodies would overheat. Having no fur enables sweat to cool the skin—and, thus, the body—directly and effectively. In our ancestors' new broiling environment, the benefits of keeping cool in the daytime would have outweighed the problem of poor insulation at night. Meanwhile, our primate cousins never left the cool jungles, so they never made the shift to hairlessness.

Humans retained the hair on their heads, it seems, because these locks help to keep the brain cool—when the sun beats down on our heads, it heats up the outermost layer of hair rather than fry the scalp directly. As for the stuff on our armpits and around our groins, the leading theory is that this hair accentuates pheromones (chemicals that are supposed to entice the opposite sex through the sense of smell). Who knew that B.O. is sexier than perfume and cologne?

Q: Why is a white flag a symbol of surrender?

A: It seems like a cliché straight out of a 1950s B-movie or an episode of *Hogan's Heroes*. Despondent and fearing for their lives, the vanquished search desperately for anything white—a handkerchief, a shirt, a pair of underpants—and attach it to a stick. They then proceed cautiously (or, in the case of Hogan's Heroes, clumsily) toward their gloating foe.

In reality, the tradition of the white flag as a symbol of surrender or truce goes back a couple of thousand years. In the West, the Roman historian Tacitus mentioned a white flag of surrender that was used at the Second Battle of Cremona in AD 69. In the East, the use of a white surrender flag is believed to date back just as distantly.

It's unclear how the color white first came to symbolize surrender. Flag experts surmise that it happened because white is a neutral hue, one that could be easily distinguished from the colorful banners that armies often carried into battle. Today, the use of the white flag as a sign of peace or surrender is an official part of the rules of warfare, as referenced in the Geneva Conventions.

The white flag has had other military uses throughout history, though none lasted long. For a short time during the Civil War, the Confederacy used a mostly white national flag that was known as the "Stainless Banner"—however, it caused confusion in battle and was scrapped. During the sixteen hundreds, the French (those lovable contrarians) used a white flag to signify the intent to go to battle. Historians don't tell us whether the French looked with disdain at anyone who didn't understand their unconventional use of the white flag—but we can guess that they did.

Q: Why don't school buses have seatbelts?

A: No, it is not for freedom of movement while aiming a spitball. Buses are actually quite safe, thanks to a design that helps make up for the lack of seatbelts. Adding seatbelts wouldn't make them much safer, as it turns out, and would actually introduce some tricky challenges.

School buses are the safest way for a child to get to school—safer than walking, riding a bike, and, yup, being driven by a parent. More than forty-two thousand people die in motor-vehicle accidents every year, according to the National Highway Traffic Safety Administration (NHTSA), but on average only six children die in school-bus accidents. Teens who drive themselves to school are one hundred times more likely to be killed than if they rode the bus. Why are children safer on the bus? Buses are bigger and higher than most other cars on the road, and they move at slower speeds. School buses also employ a safety feature called "compartmentalization."

Compartmentalization describes the little nooks and crannies that bus seats create. The seats are firmly anchored, have high backs, are filled with impact-absorbent material, and are spaced closely together. This creates individual spaces that, for the most part, keep children from being thrown forward; the kids just ricochet between the two seats. The study that suggested this form of compartmentalization was conducted in 1967 by UCLA engineers. The researchers advised using seat backs eight inches higher than what buses ended up with. They also suggested a side-padded bar to help with side collisions and rollovers, as well as a lap belt. So, the current design isn't as safe as it could be.

The NHTSA did a study that found seatbelts would reduce the annual number of fatalities by one. But lap belts alone would cause more injuries to the neck and head if they were not worn properly, which brings up another issue: Who's going to be responsible for making sure that the seatbelts are adjusted and worn correctly? A single bus driver can't make sure that fifty students are wearing their belts correctly. It isn't an efficient use of time, and those drivers put up with enough already. Seatbelts add thousands of dollars to the cost of a bus (just ask California, New York, New Jersey, and Florida, the four states that have laws requiring belts on new buses).

The most dangerous part of riding the bus is getting on and off. According to the NHTSA, four times more kids are killed outside the bus than inside—by either the bus itself or a car that didn't stop for the bus. Seatbelts wouldn't reduce this number.

Seatbelts also wouldn't reduce instances of sitting in gum, getting your hair pulled, or being called names. They could, however, reduce the incidents of one kid giving another a wedgie, so maybe they are worth additional consideration.

Q: Why is the sky blue?

A: What if the sky were some other color? Would a verdant green inspire the same placid happiness that a brilliant blue sky does? Would a pink sky be tedious for everyone except girls under the age of fifteen? What would poets and songwriters make of a sky that was an un-rhymable orange?

We'll never have to answer these questions, thanks to a serendipitous combination of factors: the nature of sunlight, the makeup of Earth's atmosphere, and the sensitivity of our eyes.

If you have seen sunlight pass through a prism, you know that light, which to the naked eye appears to be white, is actually made up of a rainbow-like spectrum of colors: red, orange, yellow, green, blue, and violet. Light energy travels in waves, and each of these colors has its own wavelength. The red end of the spectrum has the longest wavelength, and the violet end has the shortest.

The waves are scattered when they hit particles, and the size of the particles determines which waves get scattered most effectively. As it happens, the particles that make up the nitrogen and oxygen in the atmosphere scatter shorter wavelengths of light much more effectively than longer wavelengths. The violets and the blues in sunlight are scattered most prominently, and reds and oranges are scattered less prominently.

However, since violet waves are shorter than blue waves, it would seem that violet light would be more prolifically scattered by the atmosphere. So why isn't the sky violet? Because there are variations among colors that make up the spectrum of sunlight—there isn't as much violet as there is blue. And because our eyes are more sensitive to blue light than to violet light, blue is easier for our eyes to detect.

That's why, to us, the sky is blue. And we wouldn't want it any other way.

Q: Why do the Amish keep telephones outside their homes?

A: The Amish are an integral part of highway billboard culture and handcrafted furniture lore throughout Pennsylvania and parts of the Midwest. Some people know them from the 1985 Harrison Ford movie *Witness*. You remember that one, right? Ford works undercover in an Amish community to crack a murder case.

Anyway, as the movie also depicts, the Amish are a community of veritable Luddites, eschewing modern technology for the simpler pleasures of horses, buggies, and sweet, sweet beards. So the question isn't so much, "Why do Amish keep telephones outside their homes?" It's, "Why do the Amish keep telephones anywhere?"

To answer this, we'll need to understand a little bit more about the Amish than Harrison Ford films or country cookin' ads can offer. The Amish are part of a larger religious group known as the Anabaptists, which also include Mennonites and Brethren sects. In the late seventeenth century, Jakob Ammann, a Mennonite from Switzerland, led a split from the larger Mennonite church. (He felt it was getting too undisciplined.) By the early eighteenth century, members of his sect—known as the Amish—were coming to America to escape religious persecution, eventually settling in southeastern Pennsylvania.

Though the religious differences between Amish and other Christians are somewhat arcane, the Amish's views on culture and technology are what capture the public imagination. These beliefs stem from a central guiding principle known as *Gelassenheit*, which roughly means "yielding completely to God's will." Because the Amish see family structure, prayer, humility, and pacifism as the means to *Gelassenheit*, possessing most types of technology is banned. The belief is that modern-day gadgets distract people from their families and God.

Many Amish orders, however, do allow the limited use of technology (which is why you may see Amish flying on planes or taking trains). This is where telephones come in. When telephones were introduced to the Amish in the late nineteenth century, they were looked at with severe disapproval. Elders were concerned with the lascivious messages younger Amish might pass along to each other over the privacy of the phone lines, and they also worried about the spiritual implications of this "magic" form of communication.

Around 1910, the Amish community officially banned the ownership of telephones. But though the Amish may be stuck in the old ways, they aren't stupid. Telephones are incredibly practical devices, especially in the rural areas where the Amish usually live. That's why Amish leaders didn't ban the use of telephones. They allow community phones: single telephones kept in wooden shacks and shared by a number of families. These phones usually have unlisted numbers and are used for emergencies, not chit-chatting with the neighbors.

But perhaps the most important reason the Amish allow telephones in the community is also the most obvious: How else are they going to call their friends when Harrison Ford shows up to help them raise a barn?

Q Why do snakes shed their skin?

A All kinds of animals shed their skin, not only snakes. It's just that most species have the decency to do it in a less off-putting manner. Take humans. We shed about 1.5 million skin cells every hour, creating a new skin surface every twenty-eight days or so. But you don't see us walking around with huge pieces of dead skin hanging from our limbs—thank goodness for Vaseline Intensive Care.

The human skin-shedding process is ongoing, gradual, and relatively unnoticeable, while snakes shed quickly and completely, often in one long piece. Why do they do it that way? Sometimes it's to heal from an injury or remove parasites, but most of the time it's to accommodate growth. Most snakes shed at least four times over the course of a year. During the first few years of life, young snakes grow rapidly, so they shed more frequently. Before a snake sheds, it tends to lay low for a week or two. During this period of inactivity, its eyes turn a cloudy, bluish-white color, and its vision is impaired. This tends to make a snake a bit nervous and unpredictable, so beware of any snake giving you a dull, blank stare.

After seven to fifteen days, the snake's eyes return to normal, and the skin shedding begins. The first skin to be dislodged is around the head, mouth, and nose (known as the rostrum). After that, the snake starts slinking around and between rough objects like branches and rocks to help it glide out of the old skin. This can take from a few hours to a few days, depending on environmental conditions and the health of the snake.

The discarded skin of a snake can look like a dry, transparent tube or a moist, crumpled heap. Take a close-up peek at the head portion, and you'll see that a snake sheds everything—even its eye caps. One thing to note if you ever come across a snake's old skin: They often defecate at the same time they shed, so unless you're wearing gloves, it's wise to just look and not touch.

Q Why do you remember some things and forget other things?

A The short answer: No one knows for sure. Cracking the mystery of memory is among the trickiest games in science. But neurologists do have some thoughts.

Memories are patterns of electrochemical connections between neurons. Neurons are the thinkin' nerve cells in your brain. A standard-issue human brain comes with about one hundred billion neurons, which are connected to one another at points called synapses. When you form a memory, you strengthen existing synapses and create new synapses. This fashions a connection pattern among a big group of neurons.

With so many neurons, there are virtually limitless connection patterns, which means virtually limitless possible thoughts. How these patterns add up to Grandma's casserole recipe or the plot of *Police Academy 4* boggles the mind, but that's the basic idea.

No memory is an island, however. Anything you remember is connected to other things you remember, stored as neuron-connection patterns in various places. For example, when you remember winning the big break-dancing contest, the dancing part could be in one part of the brain, the music part in another. And both could be connected to other memories of your hip-hop career, which are scattered all over the brain.

The more that memories are connected to others, the greater the likelihood that those memories will "stick." You're more apt to remember details of meeting your spouse than meeting your dry cleaner. The spouse-meeting memories connect to all kinds of other things that you remember about your spouse. The dry cleaner memories connect to a few basically identical trips to the dry cleaner. The spouse-meeting is also an emotional memory, which makes it particularly well-connected in the world of neurons. Simply put, you're more likely to stumble across a memory if it's connected to many others, especially if they involve emotion.

And the more frequently you recall something, the more likely you are to remember it. Whenever you remember something, you essentially create a new memory—a brand new version of the event that is based on your new thoughts about it. This establishes new connections, which makes it easier to recall the memory. For example, if you dial the same phone number often enough, eventually you'll memorize it because it's scrawled all over your brain.

New information is more likely to stick in your memory if it connects to information you already know. You'll remember directions to a new spot in your hometown more readily than directions in a foreign city because you already know many streets and neighborhoods in your hometown.

Paying close attention also helps, of course. When committing something to memory, your brain automatically filters out what it perceives as extraneous information. This helps keep us sane: Imagine living with the memory of every overheard checkout-line conversation buzzing in your head. But this automatic filter may also make you forget where you put your keys if you were freestyle rappin' when you set them down.

What was the question again?

Q: Why does Swiss cheese have holes?

A: Rumors continue to run rampant about this age-old question. Some say manufacturers allow mice to nibble on Swiss before packaging the cheese. Others insist crafty deli owners cut the holes by hand with their carving knives. However, both of these conspiracy theories have more holes than, well, Swiss cheese.

Truth be told—and it's a bit embarrassing—Swiss cheese has holes because it has bad gas. That's right. Those holes in your sweet, nutty Swiss are actually popped bubbles of carbon dioxide gas.

Where do these gassy bubbles come from? Well, all cheese begins with a combination of milk and starter bacteria. The type of bacteria used helps determine the flavor, aroma, and texture of the finished cheese product. In the case of Swiss, cheese-makers use a special strain of bacteria called *Propionibacter shermani*. During the curing process, when the cheese ripens, this *P. shermani* eats away at the lactic acid in the cheese curd, tooting carbon dioxide gas all the while.

Swiss cheese is a densely packed variety with a thick, heavy rind, so this built-up gas has nowhere to go. Trapped inside, the gas forms into bubbles. These bubbles eventually pop, leaving behind the characteristic holey air pockets.

In formal cheese lingo, these holes are referred to as "eyes." And the art of cheese making is such that their sizes can be controlled. By adjusting acidity, temperature, and curing time, dairies can create a mild baby Lorraine Swiss with lacy-looking pinholes or a more assertive Emmentaler Swiss with eyes the size of walnuts.

Oddly, in the United States, the size of Swiss cheese holes is subject to United States Department of Agriculture regulation. Every wheel of Grade A Swiss that is sold in America must have holes with diameters that are between three-eighths and thirteen-sixteenths of an inch.

All of this goes to show that sometimes, it's best not to over-think your cheese. Just slap it on a cracker, pour a glass of wine, and enjoy.

Q: Why are Mexican jumping beans so jumpy?

A: Mexican jumping beans don't really pull off the spectacular acrobatics that you see in cartoons—and unfortunately, they don't wear sombreros, grow moustaches, or shoot guns in the air. But they do move of their own accord, which ain't bad for a bean.

Of course, there's a catch—and it's a pretty substantial one: Mexican jumping beans aren't really beans at all. They're actually seed capsules with a squirmy moth larva inside. Yes, that's kind of gross.

In the spring, the jumping bean moth, affectionately known as *Cydia deshaisiana*, lays its eggs on the flower of the jumping bean shrub (*Sebastiana pavoniana*). The larvae hatch and dig into the developing soft capsules around the shrub's seeds. As each capsule grows and hardens, the larva relaxes safely inside, snacking on the seed.

This parasitic behavior keeps the capsule from doing what it's supposed to—spreading the shrub's seed to grow more shrubs. But the shrub produces enough seed capsules that moth larvae don't take over all of them. Both species are fully able to continue their reproductive cycles.

The hardened capsules fall off the shrub, and each breaks into several pieces called carpels, some of which have a larva inside. The larva spins thread on the inside of the carpel and can actually move the capsule by gripping the thread and banging its head into the side of the capsule. It does this as an instinctive reaction to heat—when you warm a jumping bean in your hand, you'll feel it squirm. It's unclear why the larvae do this, but it may be to move the carpel out of the hot sun into cooler areas.

In any case, if you warm a jumping bean in your hand and set it on a table, you might see it shift around a bit. But there's not exactly any *jumping* going on. It's enough movement to make the beans a popular novelty item, though. In the desert Rio Mayo region of Mexico where jumping bean moths and shrubs live, locals gather up the seed pods to be sold all over the world. In desert regions of Arizona, a similar species of moth burrows into the seedpods of a similar shrub, but most jumping beans come from Mexico around the city of Alamos, the "Jumping Bean Capital of the World."

So what happens to the larva next? Before it enters the pupal stage and turns into a moth, it chews an exit door into the side of the carpel, then blocks it up again with a silk thread plug. The adult moth has no teeth so it's up to the larva to prepare this easy trapdoor ahead of time.

The next spring, the moth emerges from its pupal case and pushes through the trapdoor. If the moth finds itself in its native habitat, it fulfills its destiny of mating with another moth, laying eggs on a jumping bean shrub, and dying in peace. But if the novelty trade has taken it far from home, where there are no jumping bean moths or jumping bean shrubs, it emerges to find that it has spent a year crammed in a pod for nothing. If it could jump around shooting guns in the air, would you blame it? That's a raw deal.

Q: Why do body parts "fall asleep"?

A: It happens to all of us. You get up in the middle of the night because nature is calling, but it's hard to walk because one of your feet is "asleep." As a tingling sensation shoots through your foot, you lumber toward the bathroom like Frankenstein's monster.

What's happening? It begins when a limb has had pressure exerted on it for an extended period of time, maybe from kneeling or from crossing your arms. When this happens, the nerves in the limb obviously have pressure exerted on them, too, and this prevents those nerves from sending messages to the brain and the rest of the body. Blood vessels in the limb are also squeezed, which means oxygen being carried to the nerves is blocked and never makes it. Simply put, in the airport that is your body, too much pressure cancels a lot of incoming and outgoing flights.

The brain isn't sure what's going on—some nerves aren't transmitting any information to it, while others are sending impulses erratically. As a sort of warning signal, the limb starts to tingle. It's your body's way of saying, "Get out of that kneeling position, for crying out loud, before you cause nerve damage."

Once you jostle the affected limb, the nerves begin functioning properly again. Of course, it doesn't happen instantly. The tingling sensation often intensifies and is followed by a somewhat uncomfortable semi-numbness.

Why does this occur? Your nerves comprise bundles of fibers, and each transmits different signals to the brain. The fibers that control touch are among the thickest, and they're the last to "wake up" and resume the proper firing of impulses. That's why the final feeling you have before your limb returns to normal is that odd sensation of semi-numbness, the one that makes you look like you're starring in a B-grade horror flick.

Q Why are guinea pigs used in so many experiments?

A Why do guinea pigs make such good, well, guinea pigs? The answer is simple: Even though these furry little creatures don't look like us, they have some very human physiological features.

Like humans, guinea pigs, or *Cavia porcellus,* are among the few mammals that can't synthesize their own vitamin C, and they have significant dietary requirements for potassium, folic acid, and thiamine; these traits make them useful for studies on nutrition. In addition, they're susceptible to many of the infectious diseases that plague humans. Research using guinea pigs has contributed to cures for tuberculosis, diphtheria, yellow fever, cholera, pneumonia, and several strains of typhus.

A guinea pig also has an immune system that is similar to ours, and the animal is prone to the same allergies. Guinea pigs readily succumb to anaphylactic shock, an extreme allergic reaction that can cause death if it's not treated immediately. Because of this, they have been instrumental to the development of the inhalers and other oral medications that human asthmatics rely on to breathe freely.

Guinea pig ears are set up like ours, too, which enables scientists to study ways of reducing deafness. In 1961, Georg von Békésy of Hungary won the Nobel Prize in the medical field for his pioneering research on the function of the cochlea, the inner part of the ear, using—you guessed it—guinea pigs as his initial subjects.

According to Simon Festing, director of Britain's Research Defence Society, guinea pig research has led to twenty-three Nobel prizes in medicine or physiology. You'd think that research labs would be overflowing with the critters, but guinea pigs account for only 20 percent of all lab animals in the United States and just 1.7 percent in Britain.

People who are opposed to animal research believe that guinea pigs shouldn't be in labs at all. If you're uncomfortable with the idea of animal experimentation, you'll be glad to know that veterinarian Viktor Reinhardt—lab-animal advisor to the Animal Welfare Institute of Washington, D.C.—has issued a series of guidelines, "Comfortable Quarters for Guinea-Pigs in Research Institutions," for government and university researchers. Guinea pigs, it turns out, share not just some of our physical traits, but also many of our emotional ones. In order to enjoy happy (albeit short) lives, guinea pigs require environments where they can socialize with each other. And when three's a crowd, they need quiet places to get away from it all, just like most of us do.

Outside of the lab, guinea pigs are popular pets. So on the whole, the guinea pig population of the planet is healthy and well—and thanks to these little animals, millions of people are, too.

Q: Why are most plants green?

A: Maybe they're envious of our ability to walk over to the sink and get a drink of water.

While that theory is certainly compelling, plants aren't green with envy. The green comes from a pigment called chlorophyll. Pigments are substances that absorb certain wavelengths of light and reflect others. In other words, pigments determine color—you see the wavelength of light that the pigment reflects. A plant is green because the chlorophyll in it is really good at absorbing red and blue light but lousy at absorbing green light.

You find a heaping helping of chlorophyll in plants because chlorophyll's job is to absorb sunlight for use in photosynthesis, which is the process of converting sunlight and carbon dioxide into food (carbohydrates) that plants need to survive. So, since a plant wouldn't get too far without delicious carbs, just about every plant is partially green. This isn't true across the board, though. Some plants use different pigments for photosynthesis, and there are a few hundred parasitic plant species that don't need chlorophyll because they mooch carbohydrates that are produced by other plants. But for the most part, land plants depend on chlorophyll to maintain their active plant lifestyle. And by extension, so do we, since animal life depends on plants to survive.

But why reflect green and absorb red and blue rather than the other way around? The short answer is that the red and the blue light are the good stuff. The sun emits more red photons than any other color, and blue photons carry more energy than other colors. Sunlight is abundant enough that it wouldn't be efficient to absorb all light, so plants evolved to absorb the areas of the light spectrum that offer the best bang for the buck. And it's a good thing, too: If plants needed to absorb the full spectrum of sunlight to get by, they'd be black—and the outdoors would have a gloomy tint.

Q Why do speedometers list speeds faster than you can legally drive?

A Zip along a stretch of rural Texas Interstate at eighty miles per hour and you'll be driving just about as fast as you can go anywhere in our speed-craving country without risking a ticket. But unless you're driving some kind of Yugoslavian relic, you'll still have plenty of room to inch that needle higher on your car's speedometer. Let's say your ride is a 505-horsepower Chevrolet Corvette Z06—you'll have a whopping 120 miles per hour of speed-gauge breathing room. Is Chevy begging us to break the law? Is the company all but telling us to slam the gas pedal to the floor?

Ask experts why automakers install speedometers that mock posted limits—which usually range from sixty-five to eighty miles per hour on the highway, depending on the state you're in—and you will get discussions of manufacturing efficiencies, hints of subliminal messages, and psychological explanations that offer something in between.

"It's a one-word answer: testosterone," says Alex Fedorak, a veteran of more than two decades in car-company public relations. "It's a guy thing. They want to think they can do it, even if they never do."

Less sanguine is Richard Retting, senior transportation engineer with the Insurance Institute for Highway Safety, an underwriter-industry lobbying group. "There's no reason for any car to have a speedometer that goes over eighty miles per hour because there's no place in this country you can legally drive faster than that," Retting says. "Why car speedometers go up to 120 or 140 miles per hour makes no sense—except for marketing.

"It's no secret that speed is a key strategy for marketing vehicles in this country. Someone who bought a high-horsepower, high-speed car presumably would not be happy with a speedometer that gave the impression the car would not go up to that speed, even if they never approached that speed."

Automakers cite the economic efficiency of producing a single speedometer that's good in several countries, in which speed limits may be higher or in kilometers per hour. General Motors, which builds cars for use in virtually every nation on earth, requires its speedometers to indicate true vehicle speed at all times and to reflect the top speed of the fastest-rated tire that can be used on a particular vehicle.

Betwixt talk of testosterone and tires lies the nuanced approach of Stuart Norris, who is responsible for GM's global instrument design strategies. Norris acknowledges issues of engineering and standardization, but he also waxes about speedometer aesthetics, about the way the numerals are distributed on the speedometer's face, and how large, elegant type sends one message (luxury) and starker, closely spaced markings another (sporty). And all this time, we thought a speedometer simply indicated how fast you were going. Who knew there's much more to it than that?

A speedometer that ended at, say, eighty-five miles per hour, would "look under-populated, half-baked, even childlike," Norris says. "There's a premium-ness associated with a more populated gauge." As for that final numeral, "On a vehicle that's rated for 155 miles per hour, we expect the gauge to indicate the capability of the vehicle, even though we don't expect the customer to drive that speed."

In the end, it's all about ego. A speedometer that goes up to two hundred miles per hour connotes power, even if you can never fully unleash that power.

Q: Why do doctors hit your knee with a hammer?

A: If you're naturally paranoid, you may have considered the possibility that doctors hit your knee just because they can. After all, they could do all sorts of malicious things to us in the name of health, and we would be none the wiser. But thankfully, there's a valid reason for your doctor to whack you on the knee.

The doctor is timing a stretch reflex, a type of involuntary muscle reaction. While you're sitting on a table, the doctor taps a tendon of the quadriceps femoris, the muscle that straightens your leg at the knee. This tendon stretches the muscle suddenly, and sensory neurons send a message to motor neurons in your spinal cord. These motor neurons send a signal to the muscle in your thigh, which contracts. The result is that your leg jerks forward. The reflex is highly efficient—the sensory neurons in your knee are wired directly to the motor neurons in your spinal cord that control the reaction, and the brain isn't even involved.

The body reacts this way to keep you balanced while standing and walking without your having to think about it. Putting weight on the leg as you move or shift your balance causes the muscle to contract to support you. Similar stretch reflexes make the rest of the muscles in your legs and feet do what they're supposed to, as well.

Doctors have been banging on knees to test for spinal cord and nerve disorders for more than a century. A diminished reflex reaction can indicate a serious nerve problem, such as tabes dorsalis—the slow degeneration of nerve cells that carry sensory information to the brain. So rest assured—your doctor isn't knocking your knee simply for the entertainment value.

Q: Why are some women called "catty"?

A: Just what qualifies as catlike behavior? According to the Humane Society of the United States, cats are highly territorial animals, even more so than dogs. When it comes to defending their turf, cats will hiss, swat, chase, or ambush any other feline they see as a threat.

But a cat's behavior can be pretty difficult to predict. It's not uncommon for a cat to be territorially aggressive toward one cat yet completely cordial to another. Who knows what sets off cats? One minute they're soft, purring balls of fuzz; the next they're scratching your eyes out.

Sounds a lot like the ladies at the office, huh?

Executive coach Alicia Smith says that no one ever wants to be accused of cattiness, but at one time or another, most women have probably engaged in it. She says cattiness "can include any number of unfortunate behaviors, from not saying what we really intend to say, to saying things in a harsh tone of voice. It also includes gossiping, cynical remarks, and on a grander scale, outright rudeness."

Why so much cattiness? A 2006 study on catty behavior by University of Arkansas graduate student Kristen Norwood found that women's petty, spiteful behavior is usually the result of jealousy, competition, and insecurity. The participants in Norwood's study admitted that the potential for a catty conflict—even with strangers—was frequent. And the number one reason for the dirty looks, eye rolls, and disparaging digs? Jealousy over physical attractiveness and attention from men.

"Society sets girls up to compete with each other, primarily for male attention," says Betsy Crane of the department of sociology at Indiana University of Pennsylvania. "And I think it carries over into day-to-day life."

As for catty competition on the job, Crane speculates that society is still adjusting to women in the workplace. "Women are moving into a new sphere and gaining power," she says. "Through this, though, they're having to learn how to relate to each other and to men in different ways." And you thought it all came down to simple PMS.

Q Why does a turkey have light and dark meat?

A Once a turkey has been cooked and sliced open, the color of its meat depends on what the bird was up to when it was alive and flapping. Specifically, the hue relates to what the turkey's muscles were doing.

When muscles are exercised, oxygen-rich blood is pumped through them. As a bird ages, muscles that are used often will become denser than those that are seldom used. This density is caused by an accumulation of myoglobin, a compound that enables the movement of oxygen within muscle. A turkey's breast muscles are white meat (less dense), while the leg muscles are dark meat (more dense). This tells you that turkeys are good runners but poor fliers—their leg muscles do most of the locomotive work.

And as long as we're on the subject, let's settle another long-standing question: Which of these meats is healthier? According to the U.S. Department of Agriculture (USDA), white meat is better for you than dark meat, though the margin is slim. For one ounce of boneless, skinless breast, the USDA quotes forty-six calories and one gram of fat; an ounce of boneless, skinless thigh includes fifty calories and two grams of fat.

So the next time Thanksgiving rolls around, make sure to tell your dinner companions everything that you've learned about a turkey's white and dark meat. You'll be the life of the party.

Q Why is Chicago called the Windy City?

A Chicago has its own special set of reputations. It's known for blue-collar workers, a losing baseball team, corrupt politicians, and heart-attack-inducing foods. The city also has its share of nicknames, such as the Second City and the City of Big Shoulders. For most people, though, Chicago is the Windy City. But why?

Any shivering tourist visiting downtown Chicago during the winter could justifiably assume that this nickname is descriptive of the arctic gales that whip off Lake Michigan. Helpful Chicagoans are quick to rectify this apparent misconception. They explain that Chicago is the Windy City not for meteorological reasons, but because of its great tradition of windbag politicians.

The exact phrase is said to date back to 1890, when New York and Chicago battled for the right to host the 1893 World's Fair. The bluster from Chicago politicians in support of their city's bid led Charles Dana, editor of *The* (New York) *Sun*, to urge his readers to reject "the nonsensical claims of that windy city."

For many years, this theory was accepted as fact. It was most recently rehashed by writer Erik Larson in his bestselling book about the 1893 World's Fair, *The Devil in the White City*. One minor hitch: There is no published record of such a statement attributed to Dana. According to Barry Popik, an etymologist who has tracked down the origins of many uniquely American nicknames and slang phrases, the nickname Windy City was introduced long before 1890. Popik says that the first recorded use of the nickname can be traced to 1860 and, perhaps not surprisingly, was indeed related to the strong winds that blow off the lake. In fact, according to Popik, Chicago promoted its windy reputation in an effort to sell itself as a resort destination. (Surely this was one of the least-enticing advertising campaigns in tourism history.)

Still, the theory that links the nickname to windbag politicians might have some credence. In the second half of the nineteenth century, Chicago and Cincinnati waged a fierce war of words over which of the two cities should be considered the pearl of the Midwest. (St. Louis wanted to get in on the rivalry, but it was, you know, St. Louis.) As huge numbers of Americans moved west, midwestern cities tried to lure new residents with advertising and braggadocio, a phenomenon known as boosterism.

Chicago and Cincinnati were major hog-slaughtering centers (apparently a big draw in the nineteenth century), and both boasted about their waterfront views. It didn't take long for Cincinnati newspapers to pick up on the double entendre of "windy" with regard to Chicago. Editorials in Cincinnati newspapers hammered away at Chicago's weather and the empty bluster of its boosterism, successfully saddling their rival to the north with the Windy City moniker.

At the same time, Cincinnati won a nickname that signified its meatpacking supremacy: Porkopolis. Which begs the question: Who's having the last laugh now?

Q: Why is the U.S. presidential election held on a Tuesday in November?

A: Blame it on Congress. Before 1845, the U.S. presidential election was held during the first week of December. But that year, Congress designated November as the election month for both the president and members of Congress because November's weather is typically milder than December's. This, Congress felt, would ensure a better turnout since most Americans lived in rural areas back then and had to travel long distances by foot or on horseback to reach voting sites.

Why Tuesday? Some men (only white men could vote, remember) had to leave home a day in advance. A Monday election meant leaving home on Sunday, the day of worship. Friday and the weekend were not considered good options, either—as is the case today, weekends were booked with travel, shopping, and other business. And Thursday? That was Britain's election day, and the United States didn't want its political process to resemble Britain's in any way. Tuesday and Wednesday were the only other possibilities, and Tuesday was chosen.

Does it matter which Tuesday in November? Yes. It's always the Tuesday after the first Monday, which means elections will never be held on the first day of the month. Why is this important? When the decision was made, small businesses typically closed out their October books and balanced their ledgers on the first day of November. Furthermore, November 1 is a Catholic holiday (All Saints' Day), which might have kept some men away.

The first election following the enactment of these rules took place on November 4, 1845. It wasn't a presidential contest—members of Congress were elected—but it nonetheless marked the beginning of an American tradition.

Q: Why does a nuclear explosion form a mushroom cloud?

A: Anyone who grew up during the Cold War remembers the old "duck and cover" school drill. The fire alarm would go off, and students would dive beneath their desks and curl into a fetal position. (Did anyone really believe those desks would provide protection during a nuclear attack?) In those days, the threat of nuclear war seemed very real, and nothing symbolized it more powerfully than the image of a mushroom cloud.

Of course, we could just as easily be calling it a cauliflower cloud; a raspberry cloud; or, in one of the least-catchy nicknames of the twentieth century, a "convoluting brain cloud." Each of these terms was bandied about after the first nuclear tests in the 1940s. Regardless of what it is called, the cloud formed by a nuclear explosion remains unique.

When a nuclear device is detonated, an almost incomprehensible amount of thermal energy is released, which creates a massive fireball that incinerates everything below it (as was demonstrated in Hiroshima and Nagasaki during World War II). As the fireball rises into the air, convection currents (the same physical principle that forces hot water through radiators) rush after it, sucking up debris into a column. Eventually, the fireball reaches the peak of its upward movement and expands outward, creating the mushroom-shaped head.

This physical process occurs in other forms of explosions as well, including volcanic eruptions, as anyone who has seen pictures of the 1980 eruption of Mount St. Helens can tell you. It can even be mimicked by a certain type of cloud called the cumulonimbus, which is often a harbinger of a tornado.

Nowadays, the threat of a nuclear holocaust seems minimal; one isn't likely to look out the window and see a mushroom cloud sprouting in the distance. Still, it's always a good idea to keep a school desk nearby, just in case.

Q Why do we put candles on a birthday cake?

A Are we feeling a little sensitive about the five-alarm fire that is blazing atop the buttercream frosting? Well, take heart—the tradition of lighting candles on cakes is way older than you. The custom dates back to the ancient Greeks.

It all began as an offering to Artemis, goddess of the moon. The Greeks baked round honey cakes, topped them with tapers, and placed them on the altar of Artemis's temple. When lit, the round cakes looked like—you guessed it—full, glowing moons. Back then, people believed that smoke carried their thoughts up to the gods (hence, all of the sacrificial fires). These days, we associate lighting and blowing out the candles with making a wish. But just when did candle-topped cakes become a key part of the party?

Many historians trace the modern use of candles on cakes to Kinderfest, a German birthday celebration for children that dates to the fifteenth century. In those days, people believed that children were particularly susceptible to evil spirits on their birthdays, so friends and family gathered around protectively, lighting candles on a cake to carry good wishes up to God. It was customary for the candles to remain lit all day, and the cake was served after the evening meal.

By the eighteenth century, birthday cakes and candles took on a more festive feel. The research of culinary historian Shirley Cherkasky points to a 1799 letter written by Johann Wolfgang von Goethe (one of the greatest figures of world literature) that recounts his fiftieth birthday: "When it was time for dessert, the prince's entire livery in full regalia entered, led by the majordomo. He carried a generous-size torte with colorful flaming candles—amounting to some fifty candles—that began to melt and threatened to burn down, instead of there being enough room for candles indicating upcoming years."

Well, what do you know? You and Goethe actually have something in common: birthday cakes that resemble towering infernos. But, hey, controlled fires can be really fun (just ask any pyromaniac). And perhaps that's why the German birthday cake tradition eventually made its way over to the United States. As an 1889 American style guide directed: "At birthday parties, the birthday cake, with as many tiny colored candles set about its edge as the child is years old, is, of course, of special importance."

By 1921, American candle manufacturers started advertising boxes of little candles in mixed colors. And a few years later, people all over the United States could order cake candles and candle holders from the famous Sears Roebuck catalog. But you're way too young to remember that. Right?

Q: Why do toddlers get so many ear infections?

A: To torture sleep-deprived parents? That's part of the equation, yes. Ear infections (a.k.a. otitis media) are as much a part of raising kids as mind-grating Barney sing-alongs and embarrassing public tantrums.

In the United States, ear infections are the second-most common illness for children, just behind colds. The two usually go together, in fact. For kids who are six months to three years of age, 61 percent of colds are accompanied by ear infections.

Typically, an ear infection occurs when fluid buildup and inflammation from a cold blocks the Eustachian tube, the passageway that runs between the back of the nose and throat to the middle ear. With this tube blocked, fluid in the middle ear can't escape and builds up behind the eardrum, creating an ideal breeding ground for bacteria and viruses. This happens more often in young children than adults because kids have narrower and more horizontally positioned Eustachian tubes than grownups do. As a result, it's much easier for these tubes to get blocked up. Antibiotics can solve the problem pretty quickly, though that's of little consolation to a parent who hasn't slept in two nights.

Susceptibility to ear infections is usually highest for children who are between six and eighteen months. As kids get older, the Eustachian tubes grow wider and tilt more vertically, so the possibility of getting an ear infection diminishes greatly. Fortunately, kids also outgrow Barney. We wish we could say the same for public tantrums.

Q Why is the heart associated with love?

A Who doesn't eagerly await Valentine's Day? It's a day to celebrate your true love in the name of Saint Valentine, the patron saint of lovers. That Valentine became a saint by being beaten, stoned, and beheaded is rarely considered. Unless you're in a really bad relationship, Valentine's Day is not about beheadings, but about hearts: heart-shaped flower arrangements, heart-shaped cards, heart-shaped balloons, heart-shaped boxes of chocolates, and heart-shaped candies that taste like chalk. Hearts. Hearts everywhere. There's no escaping the hearts.

Since the time of the ancient Greeks, people have associated the heart organ with love. Aristotle posited that affections were housed in the human heart. But how did the heart shape become so ubiquitous, not only on Valentine's Day but in relation to anything associated with love? Think about it for a moment—does the ♥ symbol really look anything like a human heart? Not unless you have some serious cardiac issues. In fact, the heart shape now associated with love may not have had anything to do with hearts in the first place.

There are a couple of explanations for the origin of the symbol. The first has its roots in the ancient city of Cyrene, a Greek colony located in what is now Libya. Archeologists unearthed silver coins used in Cyrene that were stamped with the shape of the seed of a now-extinct plant, silphium.

The plant was important to ancient Cyrenians—silphium was used as a contraceptive. Interestingly, the seed's depiction is almost identical to the contemporary ♥ shape associated with love. This theory holds that the use of the plant, coupled with the prevalence of its image on circulating money, led to a natural marriage of the heart shape with love (or, at least, with passion).

This is an intriguing explanation, but like many stories of origin, it may not be entirely accurate. More likely, the development of the heart symbol is a slower, less racy tale. In fact, the heart symbol may have its roots in ivy-leaf motifs found in ancient art. Pottery and frescoes unearthed from ancient Minos, Crete, and Afghanistan all show prominent use of the heart-shaped ivy leaf. This motif was borrowed by later artists, including religious painters and sculptors, who incorporated the heart shape into depictions of Jesus and Mary as symbols of pure, unconditional love.

Once the Sacred Heart devotion of Catholicism co-opted the symbol in the Middle Ages, it became more popularly associated with love. Shortly afterward, the heart became a standard suit on playing cards, and soon the symbol was integrated into depictions of courtly love.

When the first Valentine's Day was celebrated in the late fifth century, it was only natural to associate the heart symbol with the lovers' day. Now the symbol is linked with romantic love, relegating future generations to an onslaught of heart-shaped kitsch.

Q Why is yawning contagious?

A You may think we yawn because we're tired or bored, or because oxygen levels in our lungs are low (that's the traditional medical explanation, after all). But did you know that babies yawn in utero? (They pick up the habit as early as eleven weeks after conception.) Fetuses don't take in oxygen through their lungs, and there's no way they are tired or bored—they sleep all day, and they certainly haven't viewed enough television to have problems with attention span.

Olympic athletes have been known to yawn right before competing in events. Yawning also has been connected to certain conditions, including multiple sclerosis and penile erection. Pretty weird, huh?

Scientists don't fully understand why we yawn. Does involuntarily opening one's mouth wide serve any useful or healthful purpose? It's something of a mystery. We do know, however, that 55 percent of people will yawn within five minutes of seeing someone else do it. It's a phenomenon called "contagious yawning." Sometimes just hearing, thinking, or reading about a yawn is enough to make you unconsciously follow suit. (Did it work?) Again, scientists don't know exactly why, though they have paid it enough mind to conjure a few theories.

Some researchers hypothesize that contagious yawning is more common among the empathetic crowd. In other words, those of us who demonstrate a greater ability to understand and share other people's feelings are more likely to emulate their yawns. Makes sense.

Taking that theory one step further, Dr. Gordon Gallup and researchers at the University of Albany say that empathetic or contagious yawning evolved as a way to "maintain group vigilance." Gallup thinks yawning keeps our brains working at cool, efficient, and alert levels. So in the days of early man, contagious yawning helped raise the attentiveness and danger-detecting abilities of the whole group.

Even today, members of paratrooper regiments and airborne units report yawning together right before a jump. Could contagious yawning really be leftover hardwiring from the days of yore? Quite possibly. Other theories contend that contagious yawning may have been a more explicit form of early communication. The "herding theory" suggests humans might have used contagious yawning to coordinate their behavior. One member of the group would yawn to signal an event, as if to say, "Hey, let's to go hunt for a sabertooth tiger." And the other members in the group would yawn back to reply, "Yeah, let's go."

Humans aren't the only creatures that yawn. Foxes, sea lions, hippos, dogs, and cats are among the animals that do it. Recent studies have even demonstrated that some animals, like dogs and chimpanzees, may suffer from contagious yawning.

Q Why do radio and TV station call letters begin with W or K?

A The reason goes back nearly a hundred years, before the *Titanic* sailed or World War I was fought. In the early twentieth century, radio was a form of communication rather than entertainment. Radio, or "wireless telephony," was used to send messages from ship to shore and station to station. (The idea of broadcasting music to masses of people didn't catch on until the 1920s.)

Back then, every telegraph station had a code to identify it, and those code letters were appended to every message a station sent out. The first radio operators used telegraphic codes as well, so they adopted the practice of using "calls," or call letters, to quickly identify themselves to each other.

In 1912, the United States Bureau of Navigation standardized the practice and took over the duty of assigning call letters. There were so few stations—some on land, some on ships—that a three-letter designation could cover all of them. An international agreement assigned the first letter of each call sign to different countries. The United States got the letters N and W, as well as part of the Ks: KDA through KZZ. (Germany had KAA through KCZ, though all the Ks were reassigned to the United States in 1929.)

The United States used N to designate government stations. K was for stations on the Pacific coast and for ships in the Gulf of Mexico and the Atlantic Ocean. Originally, W was for ships on the Pacific Ocean and Great Lakes and for land stations on the East Coast. Sound confusing? Of course it was; the government was involved. To further muddle matters, the Panama Canal allowed ships to travel between the Pacific and Atlantic Oceans, so their call-sign designations became meaningless.

Then radio became an entertainment industry rather than simply a messaging system. In the 1920s, radio exploded in popularity, and call signs were expanded to four letters instead of three in order to cover all the new stations. And that was just AM radio.

When FM radio and television stations were added to the mix, the Federal Communication Commission decided to stay with the K and W. It simply added an FM or TV to the end. When some

Q: Why do parents give their kids names that no one can pronounce or spell?

A: For many years, we've relied upon celebrities to give their children the types of bizarre names that leave the rest of us scratching our heads. Examples abound—from Frank Zappa's kids Moon Unit and Dweezil to Lisa Bonet's son Nakoa-Wolf Manakauapo Namakaeha Momoa. But much like tattoos and body piercings, funny-sounding baby names aren't just for celebrities anymore.

Names have always been subjected to the ever-shifting whims of fashion, although the most popular monikers for boys remain more stable than those for girls. According to the Social Security Administration, Michael ranked as the top name for boys from 1961 to 1998; Jacob ascended to the top spot in 1999 and maintained it through 2007. During that same period, Mary, Lisa, Jennifer, Jessica, Ashley, and Emily all spent time atop the girls' chart.

But recent trends have changed the game—not the names themselves, but the way they're chosen. In 1880, 41 percent of boys and 23 percent of girls were given names that were among their gender's ten most popular; by 2006, those figures had fallen to 9.5 percent for boys and 8 percent for girls. Modern parents want their children's names to be unique, for a variety of reasons.

A mother who named her daughter Jennifer in 1975 surely knew that she was choosing a popular name, but she didn't have the resources to obsess about it—there are only so many books of baby names in the library, after all.

But the mother of today has a vast sea of knowledge right at her fingertips; five minutes of Googling will reveal that her personal list of potential names is much less distinctive than she had hoped. In 2008, this realization led one Kansas couple to eschew tradition entirely, naming its daughter Gaea Althea Emma Ana Margherita VII Kaos.

Then there's the corporate-branding approach, which is supposedly a way to differentiate your offspring in the marketplace, giving them a competitive advantage over their more boringly named peers. Names chosen this way aren't hard to pronounce or spell, but they're still plenty weird. A professional baby-name consultant (yes, this is an actual occupation) told *The Wall Street Journal* that he named his son Beckett because the "C-K sound is very well regarded in corporate circles." (We here at Q&A headquarters are all a little worried for young Beckett.)

But if all parents want to give their children unique names, it will create a paradox—having a one-of-a-kind name will eventually become as common and mundane as leftover tuna casserole on a Tuesday night. When everyone has a different name, no one's name will stand out.

Which means that when it comes time for Gaea Althea Emma Ana Margherita VII Kaos to follow in her parents' footsteps and give her children the wildest, most unusual names she can think of, she'll probably choose Michael and Mary.

Why does a seashell sound like the ocean?

Is that big spiral conch you picked up during last year's trip to Hawaii still whispering sweet nothings in your ear? Well, that isn't the roar of the blue Pacific you hear—it's nothing more than the barrage of ambient noise around you.

Ah, science can be so harshly unsentimental sometimes! Seashells don't really create any sound all by themselves. Inside, they're a labyrinth of hollow areas and hard, curved surfaces that happen to be really good reflectors of racket.

When you hold a seashell up to your ear, that shell is actually capturing and amplifying all the little noises occurring around you. These noises are usually so hushed that you don't even hear them unless you're paying very close attention. However, when they begin bouncing off the cavity of a shell, the echoes resonate more loudly into your ear. And what do you know? They sound a lot like ocean waves rolling up to shore.

It doesn't matter how far away you are from the sea, or even if you have a seashell. You can recreate the same "ocean sound" effect by simply cupping your hand, or a coffee mug, over your ear. Just be sure that mug is empty—or you'll really hear a splash.

Why do you always wake up just before you die in a dream?

The answer to this question is obvious if you've seen Wes Craven's *A Nightmare on Elm Street*. Remember the main character, Freddy Krueger? Bad acne, needed a manicure—yeah, that guy. As Freddy (or more accurately, his victims) taught us, if you die in your dreams, you die in real life. There's your answer. Next question, please.

Wait, what's that? Craven isn't an authority on dream psychology? Movies aren't real?

Sorry to disappoint. Millions of children were frightened out of their pajamas by Freddy Krueger in the 1980s, but one of the underlying premises of the film and its seemingly endless stream of sequels—that dying in dream reality causes death in waking reality—has zero basis in fact. Still, the myth Craven tapped into has persisted for a long time. One of the reasons is that for many people, the dream world is as terrifying—and about as well understood—as death itself. And it follows a certain logic: After all, other dreams can affect our physical self, such as...well, you know what kind.

Another reason for the myth is that most people don't die in their dreams. Oh, they get close. But most people, whether they're plunging from the fiftieth story of a building or about to be hacked apart by fingernail blades, wake up just before the moment of truth. In fact, the dream of falling to certain death only to wake up just before impact is so common that it appears in just about every dream-analysis manual out there.

Dream experts have been somewhat baffled by this phenomenon. Although they haven't come up with a definitive explanation, some theorists believe it may have to do with myoclonic jerks. No, not your idiot neighbors who crank Metallica at three in the morning—myoclonic jerks are involuntary spasms of the muscles that jolt you out of sleep. These jerks most often strike just as you're drifting off to sleep (usually accompanied by a falling sensation), but they can also occur during rapid eye movement (REM) states.

Like many sleep and dream phenomena, researchers aren't sure what causes myoclonic jerks. One theory holds that as your body drifts into sleep, the brain mistakes the total relaxation of the muscles as a loss of bodily control. In a desperate but misguided attempt to regain control, the brain rouses the body into a conscious, hyperalert state. As we know from our pubescence, the body can't always tell the difference between dreams and reality, so it would hold that an intense dream, especially one that involves death, might induce one of these myoclonic jerks, waking you up just in the nick of time.

The death-by-dreaming myth unravels even more with a cursory glance through the annals of dream research. Numerous subjects have reported dying in dreams and waking up the next day to tell about it. So all of those folks who have been terrified by *A Nightmare on Elm Street* don't need to fret about Freddy Krueger invading their dreams. It's those people under the stairs they should be worried about.

Q: Why do round pizzas come in square boxes?

A: Here's a question that comes up virtually every time we order a pizza—which, considering our waistlines, is far too often.

According to pizza-packaging historians (yes, they do exist), the first pizza boxes were probably developed after World War II, when the popularity of takeout pizza rose dramatically. The first boxes weren't really boxes at all, but pizza placed on chipboard or corrugated cardboard and slid into a paper bag, which was subsequently taped or stapled shut. (Some longtime pizzerias still use this method.) There were a number of obvious drawbacks to this method. First, a paper bag doesn't retain heat very well, so unless you brought the pizza straight home, you'd find a congealed mess. Second, the paper bag tended to stick to the top of the pizza, so you needed to pry half of the toppings off the paper before eating the congealed mess. Third, there was no way to stack the pizzas if you were trying to carry more than one.

Pizza vendors looked for an answer—and they looked hard. Enter the square cardboard box. Though the first pizza boxes looked more like bakery boxes—you know, those flimsy white boxes that usually hold sheet cakes decorated with massive blue flowers—the corrugated cardboard box of modern times soon became the package of choice. When Domino's Pizza began in 1960, the proprietors chose these square boxes as the basis for their pizza delivery system. Square boxes provided many advantages: They were easy to stack, they were durable, and they kept the pizza warm longer.

Nowadays, square boxes persist for a number of reasons. From a marketing perspective, a square box provides the illusion of a larger, better-value pizza. (Indeed, when Domino's experimented with an octagonal box in the 1990s, rival Pizza Hut immediately launched an ad campaign claiming that Domino's was "cutting corners.") In addition, a square box provides more square footage for advertising and logo display.

Finally, we are a nation that enjoys dipping sauces. Where in a circular box do you expect pizza makers to put our dipping sauces? We need our dipping sauces! Speaking of which... where is that pizza guy?

Q: Why are reflections in a mirror reversed?

A: When you look at your reflection, you see a person with the same top and bottom as you. The head and bejeweled tiara are up high, and the feet and cowboy boots are down low. But when you raise your right hand, your reflection raises its left hand. When you pick your left nostril, your reflection picks its right. Is the man in the mirror just being contrary? Why does the mirror flip things left to right but not up to down?

Simply put, it doesn't—a mirror doesn't flip things left to right. A mirror only reverses in and out—depth—while leaving everything else intact. But as you'll discover, the depth inversion fools your brain into thinking that it's really left and right that get switched.

You can envision this depth inversion more clearly when you see a reflecting surface from an angle other than straight-on. Imagine an idyllic nature scene—a happy little tree reflected in a lake. When you compare the real tree to its reflection, you'll notice that the right-hand branches of the real tree show up on the right-hand side of the reflected tree—it's just that the reflection is upside down, inverted. It's almost as if somebody grabbed the top of the tree and pulled it straight down, through the trunk, the way you would invert a reversible poncho.

Now imagine, as you look into the mirror, that somebody did the same thing to you. (Ouch!) This is essentially what your reflection is—a version of you with your depth, relative to the mirror, perfectly inverted. So why does it seem like left and right are switched? When you stand to the side of a mirror and watch someone looking at his or her reflection, the relationship between the real person and the inverted image is clear, because you've got a good view of both. But when you're gazing lovingly at your own reflection, it's not as obvious. Your reflection looks a lot like you, not like the horrible, depth-inverted freak that it is. So instead of thinking of the reflection's right hand as an inverted version of your right hand, you imagine yourself standing as the reflection is standing—and you think of your reflected right hand as a left hand.

You can see that this is the case with a simple thought experiment. Imagine you're facing north and looking into a mirror. Point east and your reflection points east. Point up and your reflection points up. But point north—toward the mirror—and your reflection points right back out at you—south. It's only in and out that are flipped.

Now stop staring at your reflection and give somebody else a chance, you freakin' narcissist.

 Why is the day after Thanksgiving called Black Friday?

For most sane, rational humans, the day after Thanksgiving is best spent in the comfort and quiet of home. They know that venturing out can quickly turn into a nightmare. The stores open at 4:00 AM, but even this isn't early enough for the mindless consumers who camp out overnight in frigid weather to get a first crack at discounts on the gifts du jour. Escalators are jammed, grown adults shove each other out of the way to get to the toy section, and parking lots resemble a bumper car rink at the county fair.

This orgy of consumerism is popularly termed Black Friday, and anybody unfortunate enough to have to travel—or God forbid, run errands—on the day after Thanksgiving can appreciate the appropriateness of such a sobriquet. Nothing can more aptly describe the mood of somebody caught in post-Thanksgiving traffic.

Where the term "Black Friday" originated is the subject of a couple of theories. The one most commonly given in filler newspaper articles is that this is the busiest shopping day of the year and pushes retail stores into profitability—or, in accounting terms, into the black.

It's a pithy explanation, but there's no real evidence to support it. Indeed, according to the International Council of Shopping Centers, the day after Thanksgiving isn't the busiest shopping day of the year; that honor is usually reserved for one of the days right before Christmas.

The true origin of Black Friday is rooted in a deeper tradition than post-holiday sales. The concept of terming days of the week as "black" dates back to at least the Fisk-Gould scandal of 1869, when on September 24—known as Black Friday—plunging gold prices left many investors ruined. The same type of color coding was used again during the 1929 stock market crash, when not one, not two, but three days were black—Black Thursday, Black Monday, and Black Tuesday—and history books are filled with photos of Wall Street investors cramming the streets during this economic disaster. It's possible that this imagery led to the current usage of Black Friday.

According to dialect historians, the day after Thanksgiving was called Black Friday in the mid-1960s by Philadelphia policemen who dreaded the vast, slavering crowds that they were sure to encounter. Black Friday took on an even darker connotation on the day after Thanksgiving in 2008. Shoppers at a Wal-Mart in Valley Stream, New York, were so impatient to get to the bargains that they broke down the doors and shoved their way into the store, trampling an employee to death.

Q: Why doesn't the United States use the metric system?

A: For many Americans who have driven into Canada, the most immediately noticeable difference is the way things are measured. Distances are shown in kilometers and gas is sold by the liter, which can be confusing when you're used to miles and gallons. American travelers in Europe, or pretty much anywhere else in the world, face the same problem.

Why does the United States stubbornly cling to its own idiosyncratic system of weights and measures when the metric system is easier to use and universally recognized? Liberia and Myanmar are the world's only other countries that have not adopted the metric system.

Well, this turns out to be a bit of a trick question, because in many ways the United States has adopted the metric system. An 1866 law made it legal to use metric measurements in contracts and agreements. In 1893, the United States set the official definitions of U.S. units based on metric units—one U.S. pound equals 453.59237 grams, for example. And the Metric Conversion Act of 1975 (among several other laws passed over the decades) encouraged the adoption of metric units by American science and industry. For the most part, American scientists and businesses (especially those that sell goods to other countries) use the metric system every day.

What the United States hasn't done is ban the use of non-metric measuring systems. A country can pass all the laws it likes to encourage the use of a new system, but humans are naturally resistant to change. Americans like their familiar pints, yards, and acres. Until it becomes illegal to use the old system, the average American will stick with it.

In fact, even an all-metric law is no guarantee. Britain (upon whose Imperial weights and measures system the United States based its own) has been struggling with the metric system for decades. Traditionally, the British have preferred their old Imperial classifications, but their proximity to the rest of Europe has forced generations to learn both systems. Recent laws requiring the abandonment of Imperial units by shops and businesses were ignored by a few "metric martyrs," and eventually the European Union gave up trying to force the metric system on the stubborn and unwilling Brits.

So fear not, Americans—you're not in any imminent danger of losing your time-honored miles, gallons, and inches.

Q: Why do college football coaches have armed state troopers with them on the sideline?

A: A couple of state troopers are the ultimate accessories for a major-college football coach—especially in the pigskin-crazed South.

No one is certain how the tradition started, but it's usually attributed to Paul "Bear" Bryant, who was a legendary coach at the University of Alabama. The story is that Bear got a trooper entourage for security in 1958 or 1959. Not to be outdone, Ralph "Shug" Jordan, coach at Auburn University, Alabama's bitter in-state rival, secured a larger posse of troopers soon after. Let the games begin.

The tradition is both ceremonial and practical. Ceremonially, the troopers represent state pride, whether at home or away. Troopers have no law enforcement authority in another state, but armed and dressed in their official garb, they can be an imposing presence on the sideline.

From a practical perspective, the troopers' chief responsibility is to provide protection. This rarely is an issue during the game, but the playing field can fill up quickly with excited and rambunctious fans once the final seconds have ticked away. It is the job of troopers to escort the coach through the chaos to midfield for the traditional handshake with the opposing coach (who also might be flanked by troopers) and then to the locker room.

This sort of security doesn't come cheap. In 2008, ten schools in Alabama each paid the state police more than thirty-eight thousand dollars for "football detail." Some troopers in other states provide coach protection at no cost, as long as the college pays for meals and travel expenses.

The practice is nearly ubiquitous among NCAA Division I-A teams in the Southeastern Conference and has also caught on with some schools in the ACC, Big East, Big 12, and Big Ten conferences. Trooper detail hasn't taken root in the West, however—the Pacific-10 Conference is explicitly opposed to the practice. Teams that don't have trooper support generally rely on campus police for coach security.

For a trooper assigned to a coach, staying calm, cool, and collected might be the toughest part of the gig. Troopers typically are huge fans of their assigned teams, but they're expected to maintain stoic professionalism. And this is no small feat if they've just witnessed a game-winning touchdown.

Q Why are Democrats on the left and Republicans on the right?

A In this era of cable-channel charlatans, jingoist radio shows, and boorish bloggers, it's tempting to see things in black and white. In political discourse, this polarization finds expression in the terms "left" and "right."

Regardless of what their respective defenders and detractors might like to believe, "right" in this sense isn't a synonym for "correct." And "left" doesn't conjure up the bogeyman—even if our word "sinister" does come from *sinestra si*, Latin for "left."

The concept of the political "left" and "right" can be traced across the Atlantic Ocean to France. It came to the fore in 1789 during the French Revolution, when the National Assembly first convened. The Assembly consisted of three groups, known as "estates." The first estate was the clergy, the second the nobility, and the third the commoners. (The term "fourth estate," which is used to describe journalism, has its roots here.)

These estates did not get along particularly well. During meetings, the first and second estates began to congregate on the right side of the chamber; the third estate tended to sit on the left. This ad hoc arrangement became the norm over the course of the Revolution.

As one might expect, the clergy and nobility—the right—were pretty happy with the way things were: They were conservative toward change to the status quo. By contrast, the commoners—the left—were tired of suffering at the hands of the wealthy: They were liberal toward change.

This ideological bifurcation was brought to the English-speaking world's attention in Thomas Carlyle's popular 1837 treatise on the French Revolution. It was soon adopted by political pundits in Britain, even though Parliament had no such seating chart.

During the nineteenth century, the concept of a political right and left moved across the pond to America. It became shorthand for the conservatism we ascribe to Republicans and the liberalism with which we characterize Democrats.

The reality, of course, is more nuanced, but broadcast blowhards work best in black and white.

Q: Why is it called a honeymoon?

A: The word "honeymoon" has come to refer to the oh-so-brief period of bliss before a new Mister and Missus take on the daunting task of holding their marriage together. Once the vows are exchanged, it's only a matter of time before someone's saying, "Looks like the honeymoon is over." In other words, the real work has begun.

The first printed reference to a honeymoon came in 1552, by Richard Huloet. In his usage, the word recalled the sweetness of honey and the ephemeral quality of the moon—as in, "revel in your marital bliss now, because it isn't going to last." Just as the moon waxes and wanes, so too do the geniality and love in a marriage. It's easy to read this interpretation as cynical, but it doesn't have to be. As writer Paula Guran points out, the moon always waxes again after it wanes.

There are other potential origins of the term, but they lack substantial evidence. One of these goes all the way back to the days of the Vikings and is based on little more than the word's incidental similarity to the Norse word for "hiding." This theory suggests that "honeymoon" refers to the time that a man would spend with a kidnapped woman from a neighboring village, in hiding from the kinfolk of his stolen "wife."

So grab your goblet of mead, take your kidnapped bride by the waist, and make the most of your time in seclusion. Before you know it, her angry brothers will stop searching for her, the intoxication will wear off, your stay in the hotel room with the balcony overlooking Niagara Falls will come to an end, and you'll be forced to reenter the real world.

Q Why do phone numbers on TV shows and in movies start with 555?

A In 1988, the British pop band Squeeze released a single called "853-5937." The phone number in the title had once belonged to the band's lead singer, Glenn Tilbrook, and the song was based on a jingle that he had used on his answering machine.

The single climbed the charts and became one of Squeeze's few U.S. hits. Good news for the band; bad news for anyone else who happened to have that phone number. Around the country, annoyed citizens reported receiving up to fifty calls a day from fans hoping to speak to members of Squeeze. Some of the callers became combative when told that no one from the band was at that number—never mind that the members of Squeeze lived on an entirely different continent.

And this, in a nutshell, is why phone numbers referenced in TV shows and movies usually start with 555: As the Squeeze example illustrates, a surprising number of people are idiots. The moment that a phone number is mentioned—even in passing—on any television show or movie, you can rest assured that some moron is frantically punching the numbers into his phone. (The same thing happened in 1980 when the band Tommy Tutone hit number four on the charts with a song that had the number 867-5309 in its chorus.)

So what makes 555 numbers immune to this problem? For years, numbers beginning with 555 had been reserved by the phone company for special use—most notably, 555-1212 for directory assistance. Few other 555 numbers had ever been assigned, so scriptwriters felt comfortable using made-up 555 numbers to idiot-proof their productions.

In 1994, the agency that assigns phone numbers—the North American Numbering Plan Administration—decided to start offering 555 numbers to the general public. The idea was to turn the 555 exchange into something like the 800 prefix—easily accessible from any area code and (theoretically) attractive to businesses that wanted easy-to-remember phone numbers.

Mindful of the ever-present danger of idiots, the administrators reserved a range of numbers—555-0100 to 555-0199—for use in works of fiction. Potential problems solved.

Back to Squeeze. For what it's worth, the pop band despised "853-5937" about as much as the unwitting victims of the song did. "I hold myself solely responsible for this utter waste of time," Tilbrook would declare years later in the book *Squeeze: Song by Song*. That said, he did relish the annoyance that his song created: "We made the front page of *USA Today* because so many irate people were getting calls. That was the only good thing about the song."

Q: Why do they call it the Dark Ages?

A: Okay, so maybe the Roman Empire crumbled and all of its advances in urban refinement—in fundamental areas such as agriculture, roads, and sanitation—fell into steep decline.

So maybe a few Germanic tribes accosted southern and western Europe and wreaked a little havoc on the culture and the social order. So maybe there was a plague. The truth is, anyone can have a bad half-millennium. Do we have to rub salt into the wounds and call the whole messy affair the Dark Ages? Is that really fair?

Actually, modern-day historians generally don't use that term anymore. The period that ran from roughly AD 500 to 1000 is now referred to in less pejorative terms, such as "Late Antiquity" or the "Early Middle Ages." For a while, the term "Dark Ages" was co-opted from its original, negative meaning and was used to refer to the fact that historical detail of the era was a bit sketchy—but that never really caught on.

The notion of a specific period of time that we now know as the Middle Ages originated with Renaissance historians. As the Renaissance got into full swing in the fourteenth century, Italian humanist historians sought to link their movement with the classical philosophical movements of Rome and Greece (beginning around the fifth century BC). They needed a name for the downtime between the two movements, so they called it "the Dark Ages," thumbed their noses at it, and then went about the task of showing how enlightened they were.

Fourteenth-century Italian poet-scholar Petrarch is said to have coined the term "Dark Ages." It doesn't appear that he actually used that exact phrase himself, but he is still credited with introducing the idea of a time when knowledge of the great works of classical antiquity faded into obscurity, with nothing new being offered in its place—even if modern historians strenuously disagree with his dismal assessment.

Q: Why do trees lose their leaves?

A: Trees that lose their leaves in the colder months are of the deciduous variety. The term "deciduous" comes from the Latin *deciduus*, which means "that which falls off." Fancy schmancy evergreens, on the other hand, get to keep their leaves all year long.

Deciduous trees lose their leaves in the winter for the same reason that bears hibernate: It's all about conserving energy. In the summer, leaves absorb nutrients from the sun; through photosynthesis, they provide the tree with energy. But as the days get shorter and there's less sunlight available, leaves suddenly become a tree's jobless friends, mooching off the tree's water supply without giving much back.

And as it turns out, these suddenly useless leaves could also pose a big safety risk for the tree during winter. Everybody's seen a tree's branches sag when they're coated with ice; if there were leaves on those branches, there would be more surface area on which frost could form and, thus, a greater chance of breakage. The additional surface area would also mean that the tree would lose more moisture to cold wind. So the tree goes naked for the winter and stores the water it needs in its trunk and branches.

But how does it happen? When the tree sets its clock back to standard time, so to speak, it begins to kick the leaves to the ground by releasing the hormones ethylene and abscisic acid. Meanwhile, two other chemical compounds—auxin and cytokinin, which are a tree's growth hormones—diminish in proportion. The leaf-dropping process continues as ethylene and abscisic acid build up a corklike material in the leaf's separation layer, which is between the leaf and the branch. The accumulation of these corky cells in the separation layer keeps any water from getting to the leaf and prevents its sugar from escaping. While the separation layer is disintegrating, a protective layer of cells forms on the tree at the leaf's base. When this process is complete, the leaf falls off. Multiply that by several hundred or thousand leaves, and you have a tree that is ready for winter.

Finally, of course, trees lose their leaves in order to provide children with giant piles to jump in. But take notice: None of these leaves are oak leaves—the separation layer of the mighty oak never deteriorates enough to allow its dead leaves to fall.

Q Why does the American flag have stripes?

A The American flag is one of the most recognizable symbols of the United States, with its fifty white stars set against a blue field and its thirteen horizontal stripes of alternating red and white. Known variously as "Old Glory," "The Star-Spangled Banner," and "The Stars and Stripes," the U.S. flag has undergone a number of design changes over the course of American history. The stripes, however, have pretty much remained in place from the beginning.

Although it's unclear who originally designed the flag, evidence suggests that it was Francis Hopkinson, a signer of the Declaration of Independence, in the late 1770s. Today, each of the flag's fifty stars represents a state. (The number of stars has accounted for most of the revisions to the flag, as the count had to be updated every time a new state joined the union.) Originally, the stripes followed the same concept: Each stripe was to represent a colony, and that number was thirteen when the nation was born.

The Flag Act, dated June 14, 1777, laid out the initial guidelines for flagmakers: "Resolved, that the flag of the United States be thirteen stripes, alternate red and white; that the union be thirteen stars, white in a blue field representing a new constellation." In May 1795, the numbers were changed to fifteen stars and fifteen stripes, but a later act, signed in 1818, established the format we have today: The flag would have no more than thirteen stripes, but a star would be added for each state in the union.

Thank goodness for the limit on stripes. Imagine the consequences if there weren't: The flag would either be three stories high or have stripes so thin that you'd need a magnifying glass to tell one from another.

Q: Why are people afraid of clowns?

A: Got a case of coulrophobia? You're not alone. Experts estimate that as many as one in seven people suffer from an abnormal or exaggerated fear of clowns. The symptoms of this strangely common affliction range from nausea and sweating to irregular heartbeat, shortness of breath, and an overall feeling of impending doom. Is the sight of Ronald McDonald more chilling than your Chocolate Triple Thick Shake? There could be a few reasons why.

The most common explanation for coulrophobia is that the sufferer had a bad experience with a clown at a young and impressionable age. Maybe the clown at Billy Schuster's fifth birthday party shot you in the eye with a squirting flower, doused your head with confetti, or accidentally popped the balloon animal he was making for you. Some of the most silly or mundane things can be petrifying when you are young. And though the incident may be long forgotten, a bright orange wig or bulbous red nose might be enough to throw you back into the irrational fears that plagued your younger days.

Who could blame you? If television and movies have taught us anything, it's that clowns often are creatures of pure evil. There's the Joker, Batman's murderously insane archenemy; the shape-shifting Pennywise from Stephen King's *It*; the human-eating alien clowns in *Killer Klowns from Outer Space*; and a possessed toy clown that comes to life and beats the bejesus out of a young Robbie Freeling in Steven Spielberg's *Poltergeist*.

Real-life serial killer John Wayne Gacy didn't do much for the clown cause, either. Before authorities found the bodies of twenty-seven boys and young men in his basement crawl space, Gacy was known as a charming, sociable guy who enjoyed performing at children's parties dressed up as Pogo the Clown or Patches the Clown. That ended when his crimes were discovered, but even on death row, he still had an unwholesome interest in clowning—he took up oil painting, and clowns were his favorite subjects.

It's enough to give anyone the heebie-jeebies. But some experts say there's more to coulrophobia than traumatic childhood events or pop-culture portrayals. Scholar Joseph Durwin points out that since ancient times, clowns, fools, and jesters have been given permission to mock, criticize, or act deviantly and unexpectedly. This freedom to behave outside of normal social boundaries is exactly what makes clowns so threatening.

A *Nursing Standard* magazine interview of 250 people ages four to sixteen revealed that clowns are indeed "universally scary." Researcher Penny Curtis reported some kids found clowns to be "quite frightening and unknowable." Seems it has a lot to do with that permanent grease-painted grin. Because the face of a clown never changes, you don't know if he's relentlessly gleeful or about to bite your face off. In the words of Bart Simpson: "Can't sleep; clown will eat me."

Q: Why do marathon runners wrap themselves in foil after a race?

A: Watching thousands of marathon runners clog the streets of a major city is odd. Odder still is the sight of these runners huddled in foil wrappers after the race. What are those things anyway?

After suffering through 26.2 miles of agony on the pavement, it seems that the last thing you would need is someone packaging you up like you're about to be sold off of a downtown food cart. But in fact, you cover a runner in foil for the same reason you would a baked potato or a burrito—to keep in heat.

These foil coverings are called HeatSheets, and they can be lifesavers for people who run marathons, particularly in cold weather. Runners shed clothing as they move through a long-distance race, usually finishing in shorts and a T-shirt. The body heats up during a race and, therefore, sweats as a cooling mechanism. It's virtually impossible for a runner to drink enough liquid during a race to offset the moisture he or she loses through sweating, so dehydration sets in. This also prevents the body from cooling properly.

That's not a huge problem until the end of the race, when a runner begins to cool down—rapidly, if the weather is chilly. The cool-down can happen so quickly that it fools the body's internal sensors, which haven't gotten the message that the race is over and continue to shed heat. In such a case, dehydration quickly turns to hypothermia.

HeatSheets prevent the rapid loss of body heat. They're made of Mylar (a plastic sheeting) and coated with a thin layer of aluminum, which keeps heat trapped against the body. In addition, because of their economical size, HeatSheets are better to hand out after a race than, say, blankets or sweatshirts. They just look a lot sillier.

Q: Why do grapes spark in the microwave?

A: That's right—you can do more with your microwave than just pop corn and defrost chicken. You can cause a mini electrical storm, make a piece of fruit spontaneously ignite, and possibly create a floating plasma fireball. All you need is a bunch of grapes. Mind this caveat, however: These experiments can cause serious and even irreparable damage to your appliance. Do your family a favor—if you *must* see this for yourself, try the experiments in the microwave in the employee lounge at work, preferably while your boss is away on vacation.

Microwaves heat food by bombarding it with waves of mild radiation. When these waves come into contact with a substance that conducts electricity—such as the juice inside a grape—that substance becomes charged. If the grapes are placed close enough together, the charge will move back and forth between them. As the charge moves through the air, the air itself becomes charged, producing a light show known as "arcing."

In another variation on this experiment, a single grape is sliced in half, with a bit of skin left connecting the two halves. The electrical current produced in each section of grape will travel over this bridge, which will heat the skin and eventually cause it to catch fire. The point at which the grape starts to burn is known as "a good time to turn off the microwave." (See "serious and even irreparable damage," above.) If the reaction taking place is not stopped, the heated gas between the two grape halves could form a plasma fireball. This cloud of plasma is created by the microwave's electrical field, which feeds off the radiation inside the appliance. The radiation causes the cloud to get hotter and hotter. As this continues, the odds of your microwave surviving the experiment dwindle, so enjoy the show while you can.

Other foods have been known to produce the same effect, or a similar one: Cranberries, blueberries, and green peppers have all produced electrical arcs. Pickled cucumbers start to glow when they have been microwaved for a long enough span of time. But obviously, these experiments aren't recommended. Appliance manufacturers caution that running an empty microwave can cause major damage to the microwave tube. Running a microwave with a couple small pieces of fruit can cause the same kind of damage, if the machine is allowed to run long enough.

So wait until the boss leaves for Cancun, turn the lights down, and toss a couple grapes into the microwave. You may get fired, but at least Rod and Joey—that annoying duo from Accounting—will remember you as "the guy who got our microwave privileges taken away."

Q: Why can't you teach an old dog new tricks?

A: It's not that you can't; it's that you might face some frustration if you try. As the brain ages—whether it be a canine's or a human's—it loses neurons, or nerve cells. With fewer neurons, there are fewer connections between the neurons, and it's in these connections that your memories are stored. Before you know it, you've spent over an hour looking for your bifocals when they've been on your head the whole time.

Young people run circles around old folks in terms of short-term memory, perceptual speed, muscular strength, and physical coordination. They also have much sharper vision and hearing. But that certainly doesn't mean that a Methuselah has to throw in the towel.

"Learning a new skill, like playing the piano or speaking a foreign language, would be harder at age eighty than age eight, since all bodily processes decline as we age," says Dr. Linda Espinosa, a retired professor of education who taught at the University of Missouri-Columbia. "But it's certainly not impossible."

Okay, so maybe it's too late for Gramps to master that triple Salchow on ice. But he did learn how to get cash from the ATM and program the VCR to tape his favorite reruns of *Matlock*. And that's pretty cool.

According to John W. Rowe and Robert K. Khan, authors of the MacArthur Foundation study "Successful Aging," research shows that "older people can, and do, learn new things—and they learn them well." But it's important to be realistic: "The limits of learning, and especially the pace of learning, are more restricted in age than in youth."

Want to stay sharp as a tack well into your twilight years? Rowe and Khan say that three lifestyle features predict strong mental functions in old age: regular physical activity, a strong social support system, and a belief in your ability to deal with whatever life throws at you.

That's all well and good, but where are those car keys?

Q: Why is coffee called "joe"?

A: With the exploding popularity of gourmet coffee drinks in recent years and the vast number of specialty, fair-trade, and organic coffee purveyors now dominating the market, it's sometimes a challenge to find a joint that serves up plain old coffee. And when you do stumble upon such a place, asking for a "cuppa joe" is more likely to be met with a blank stare than a cup of coffee (unless the barista is a fan of old, hard-boiled detective movies). Yet for much of the twentieth century, coffee was indeed referred to as joe.

Why "joe"? Why not Bob? Or Fred? Or even Orville? There are a number of prevailing theories as to why coffee is referred to as joe. The first—and the one that's promoted by the United States Navy—holds that in 1913, new Navy Secretary Josephus Daniels abolished the policy of allowing sailors to drink alcohol at mess. In false praise, American sailors began referring to coffee—which now was the most powerful beverage available to them—as a "cup of joe." However, most etymologists discard this theory, pointing out that the first time that the phrase "cup of joe" appeared in print was in 1930, and a seventeen-year gap between the first colloquial use and the first recorded use is virtually unheard of.

A second explanation is only partly military in origin. The term "joe" long referred both to an average American and to an American soldier (think G.I. Joe), and because coffee is both the average man's drink of choice and a primary staple of a soldier's rations, coffee became associated with the name Joe. This makes sense, right?

The least interesting theory (but the one that's most likely correct, according to some etymologists) suggests that "joe" is a bastardization of Java, the island that for a long time was the primary source of coffee to North America. Of course, those folks who pronounced Java as "joe" might have been drinking something a lot stronger than joe. Jack, perhaps.

Q **Why hasn't anyone found a cure for the common cold?**

A For one thing, there's no such disease. The so-called common cold is actually a set of general symptoms that are associated with more than two hundred separate virus strains. The worst offenders are varieties of rhinovirus, which cause 10 to 40 percent of colds, but coronaviruses and other virus families produce their fair shares of colds as well.

When a virus infects your upper-respiratory system—by invading your body's cells and using the cells' energy to replicate itself—your immune system sends in white blood cells to fight it. If you've never been infected by that particular virus strain, the immune system doesn't know how to destroy it, so the first attack against it isn't successful. The battle rages on until your immune system figures out how to knock out the virus. The results of the fight are tissue inflammation and a lot of mucus, which cause congestion, a sore throat, coughing, a runny nose, and sneezing. All this hacking and dripping expel the virus from your body.

So finding a cure for the common cold actually means dealing with hundreds of separate viruses, some of which scientists haven't even identified yet. The good news is that once you've been infected by a virus, your immune system can usually recognize that particular strain when it shows up again and knock it out immediately. The bad news is that cold viruses keep pace with the immune system by mutating. As the virus strains change, the body doesn't recognize them anymore—it's a never-ending arms race.

Furthermore, finding a cure for the common cold isn't exactly the top priority within the medical community—researchers have bigger fish to fry, such as cancer, diabetes, heart disease, and a long list of other afflictions. Besides, people typically bounce back from a cold within a week or so.

There are, however, scientists who are working on a cure for the common cold, and they've made some progress. In February 2009, researchers from the University of Maryland and the University of Wisconsin announced that they had decoded the genome for ninety-nine strains of rhinovirus, which, as we said, is the main cold virus. They mapped the relationships among the strains as if they were assembling a family tree. This information revealed some persistent commonalities among the strains, which could pave the way for future treatments.

In the meantime, the best cure for the common cold is your immune system's attack on the virus. Or put another way, the best cure for the common cold is the common cold.

Q: Why do baseball managers and coaches wear uniforms instead of street clothes?

A: Coaches in basketball, football, hockey, and soccer are content to wear street clothes, and some, such as Pat Riley in the NBA, have even garnered extra respect for their sartorial strategies. Yet managers and coaches in baseball dress just like the players. What gives?

More than any other sport, baseball clings to its traditions—not unlike the way a stretchy polyester uniform clings to the expanding midsection of an aging manager. Despite such modern phenomena as free agency, domed stadiums, and sausage races, today's baseball culture still has roots in the game's distant past.

In the nineteenth century, ball clubs really were clubs—fraternities that played baseball by day and gathered at night for formal parties, where players ate, drank, socialized, and sang special club songs. The uniforms they wore were almost sacred articles that distinguished the players not only from those of rival ball clubs but also—and perhaps more importantly—from spectators and the rest of society at large.

In those early days, the captain of the team held the responsibilities of a modern-day manager: creating lineups, making key tactical decisions, and kicking dirt on the shoes of an unsympathetic umpire. As the game evolved and the century turned, the more successful captains found work as managers after their playing days were over. But since they were unwilling to surrender their membership in the fraternity of baseball, they continued to wear their uniforms.

There were exceptions—most famously, Connie Mack, who managed the Philadelphia Athletics for a preposterously long time, from 1901 to 1950. A former major-league player, Mack nevertheless wore a suit and tie when he managed the A's. Perhaps not coincidentally, Mack also owned the franchise, so his ties to the fraternity were likely not as strong as those of most managers.

There are some practical considerations. Many baseball coaches spend time on the field before the game instructing players, leading them in warm-ups, and hitting ground balls to infielders—all of which would be difficult to accomplish in a suit and tie.

What's more, the official rules of Major League Baseball stipulate that first- and third-base coaches should be in uniform. There's no mention of the manager, though; in fact, rule 3.15 states, in part, "No person shall be allowed on the playing field during a game except players and coaches in uniform, managers, [and] news photographers...." The rulebook seems to be saying, indirectly, that the manager doesn't need to be in uniform.

But an incident in 2007, during which a representative from the baseball commissioner's office harassed Boston Red Sox manager Terry Francona during a game for not complying with the league's dress code (Francona sometimes preferred to wear a Red Sox pullover instead of the regulation uniform top), suggests that today's baseball uniform remains every bit as sacred as the sausage race.

Q: Why are some chicken eggs white and others brown?

A: This one is easy: An egg's color is determined by the breed of hen that laid it. According to the American Egg Board, breeds with white feathers and white earlobes, such as the White Leghorn, lay white eggs; breeds with red feathers and red earlobes, such as the Rhode Island Red, lay brown eggs. It's that simple. But it doesn't answer other questions about white eggs and brown eggs.

For instance, have you heard that brown eggs are more nutritious than their white counterparts? Whoever told you that one is eleven short of a dozen. Egg color has no effect on nutritive value or on taste, quality, or cooking performance. Once you crack the shell, white and brown eggs are the exactly the same on the inside.

It comes down to personal preference. There is more demand for white eggs in most parts of the United States, so the chances are good that you'll find more of them in your grocer's dairy case. Take your cart for a spin at the Stop & Shop in Greenwich, Connecticut, however, and you may find the opposite to be true. Regionally speaking, New Englanders are partial to brown eggs.

If white eggs and brown eggs are equally good, why are brown eggs more expensive? The birds that lay brown eggs are slightly larger than their white-egg-laying counterparts. Consequently, they require more food to get a-laying, and that cost is passed on to consumers.

Before you go counting all your chickens, however, you might want to know that eggs come in colors other than just white and brown. Rare "boutique" hens, such as the Araucana, lay eggs in beautiful blue and blue-green colors. No PAAS color kit required at Easter for these eggs!

Q Why did doctors perform lobotomies?

A Few people have first-hand experience with lobotomized patients. For many of us, any contact with these convalescents comes via Hollywood—that searing image at the end of *One Flew Over the Cuckoo's Nest* of Jack Nicholson, as Randle Patrick McMurphy, lying comatose. Hopefully, we've all experienced enough to know that Hollywood doesn't always tell it like it is. After all, what would be the point of a medical procedure that turns the patient into a vegetable? Then again, perhaps this is the reason that lobotomies have taken a place next to leeches in the Health Care Hall of Shame.

What exactly is a lobotomy? Simply put, it's a surgical procedure that severs the paths of communication between the prefrontal lobe and the rest of the brain. This prefrontal lobe—the part of the brain closest to the forehead—is a structure that appears to have great influence on personality and initiative. So the obvious question is: Who the heck thought it would be a good idea to disconnect it?

It started in 1890, when German researcher Friederich Golz removed portions of his dog's brain. He noticed afterward that the dog was slightly more mellow—and the lobotomy was born. The first lobotomies performed on humans took place in Switzerland two years later.

The six patients who were chosen all suffered from schizophrenia, and while some did show post-op improvement, two others died. Apparently this was a time in medicine when an experimental procedure that killed 33 percent of its subjects was considered a success. Despite these grisly results, lobotomies became more commonplace, and one early proponent of the surgery even received a Nobel Prize.

The most notorious practitioner of the lobotomy was American physician Walter Freeman, who performed the procedure on more than three thousand patients—including Rosemary Kennedy, the sister of President John F. Kennedy—from the 1930s to the 1960s.

Freeman pioneered a surgical method in which a metal rod (known colloquially as an "ice pick") was inserted into the eye socket, driven up into the brain, and hammered home. This is known as a transorbital lobotomy.

Freeman and other doctors in the United States lobotomized an estimated forty thousand patients before an ethical outcry over the procedure prevailed in the 1950s. Although the mortality rate had improved since the early trials, it turned out that the ratio of success to failure was not much higher: A third of the patients got better, a third stayed the same, and a third became much worse. The practice had generally ceased in the United States by the early 1970s, and it is now illegal in some states.

Lobotomies were performed only on patients with extreme psychological impairments, after no other treatment proved to be successful. The frontal lobe of the brain is involved in reasoning, emotion, and personality, and disconnecting it can have a powerful effect on a person's behavior. Unfortunately, the changes that a lobotomy causes are unpredictable and often negative. Today, there are far more precise and far less destructive manners of affecting the brain through antipsychotic drugs and other pharmaceuticals.

So it's not beyond the realm of possibility that Nicholson's character in *Cuckoo's Nest* could become zombie-like. If the movie gets anything wrong, it's that a person as highly functioning as McMurphy probably wouldn't have been recommended for a lobotomy.

The vindictive Nurse Ratched is the one who makes the call, which raises a fundamental moral question: Who is qualified to decide whether someone should have a lobotomy?

Q: Why can't you tickle yourself?

A: If only bullies chose this question instead of the far more popular, "Why are you hitting yourself?" You can't tickle yourself because your brain couldn't care less about your attempts at tickling—it basically says, "Duh, I know! I told your fingers to do that." When someone else tickles you, however, the contact is unexpected, and the shock contributes to the effect.

When the nerves of your skin register a touch, your brain responds differently depending on whether you're responsible for it. MRI scans show that three parts of the brain—the secondary somatosensory cortex, the anterior cingulated cortex, and the cerebellum—react strongly when the touch comes from an external source. Think of it like this: When you see a scary movie for the first time, you jump when the maniac suddenly appears and kills the high school kids as punishment for having teenage sex. The second time you see the movie, it isn't a surprise, so you don't jump. The same goes for tickling: It's the element of surprise that causes the giddy laughter of the ticklish.

Why do we laugh hysterically when other people tickle us? Scientists believe that it's an instinctual defense mechanism—an exaggerated version of the tingle that goes up your spine when an insect is crawling on you. This is your body's way of saying, "You may want to make sure whatever is touching you won't kill you." The laughter is a form of panic due to sensory overload.

If you're in desperate need of tickling but have no friends or family willing to help, you can invest in a tickling robot. People do respond to self-initiated remote-control tickling by a specialized robot that was developed by British scientists in 1998. There's a short delay between the command to tickle and the actual tickle, which is enough to make the contact seem like a surprise to the brain and induce fits of laughter.

Now that the pressing problem of alleviating loneliness through robotic tickling has been addressed, scientists can shift their attention back to finding a cure for cancer.

Q: Why is it always the other guy who has the accent?

A: Everyone knows the United States has three dialects: New York, Southern, and normal. Regardless of where you live, you probably think that you belong to the "normal" group—even if you're from the East Coast or smack dab in the middle of Dixie.

Face it: When it comes to how we sound, we're a bit solipsistic unless we don't have a dictionary handy, in which case we're a bit self-centered. We hear those neutral-sounding voices on TV and radio and think, "Yeah, that's pretty much how I sound." And we're pretty much all wrong.

We're quick to snicker when we hear someone speaking with an accent, a "twang," or a "lilt." But no matter who you are, where you are from, or how you talk, there are a lot of Americans who, if they heard you speak, would think, "Listen to that funny accent!"

When are people secretly chuckling at your accent? Probably when you use some of the telltale words that linguists use to pinpoint dialects. When you say "pin" and "pen," do they sound the same? How about "merry," "Mary," and "marry"? When you say "about," does the ou rhyme with the ou in "loud?" (A Web search on American dialects will reveal several sites where you can take tests to identify yours. This will help you know where in the country people will laugh behind your back.)

Dialects in the United States are native to a handful of regions—North, South, and West, for example—but each contains a number of local variations. A Southern accent in Texas, for example, sounds much different from a Southern accent in South Carolina.

The accent that most people consider to be normal is sometimes referred to as the Midland dialect; it's common across Pennsylvania and Ohio and west to the Great Plains. It is closest among regional accents to that neutral sound we hear in commercials. But even Midland speakers give themselves away with similar pronunciation of such words as "cot" and "caught" or "pin" and "pen."

So the next time that you think it's the other guy who has the accent, recall the first time you heard your voice played back in a video or a sound recording. Remember how you cringed because suddenly you sounded so weird? That's because you do.

Q Why isn't anyone ever smiling in old photographs?

 To hear the older generation tell it, the world used to be a bleak, severe place. There were no televisions, no telephones, no automobiles. Dinner was a crust of bread, and chores took twenty hours a day. The wind was always gusting, the temperature was perpetually forty below, and the only direction that existed was uphill. And based on old photographs, everybody was apparently ticked off all the time.

For many years, portrait photography was a grim business. Look at almost any portrait photo from the nineteenth century—the subjects are bound to be glaring back at you, usually while in ridiculous poses and surrounded by all sorts of odd props. Part of the reason for this pomp and circumstance was that photography was a new technology at the time, but portraiture was not. Classically, portraits were never painted of a smiling subject. For one thing, it would be physically impossible to hold a smile for the hours it took to complete a painted portrait. But it was also considered silly or ignoble to be depicted with a smile. Most people who commissioned portraits of themselves wanted to be portrayed as serious and fair-minded, great leaders of men—not as drunken court jesters.

When photographic portraits became all the rage in the mid-nineteenth century, photographers and subjects maintained the tradition of somber regality. However, tradition was only part of it. There were physical limits, as well: Exposure times of early cameras could be up to several minutes. Pretending to smile for more than a minute or so becomes awfully tough on the facial muscles, as anyone who's suffered through a dinner with future in-laws can attest.

As camera technology improved and exposure times decreased, there was no longer any physical reason for portrait subjects not to smile. Still, the convention lived on in many photographers' studios, which is why there were unsmiling photographed subjects well into the twentieth century.

People who study the history of photography point to George Eastman as one of the major forces behind putting the smile into photographed portraits. Eastman, the founder of Kodak, is credited with inventing the roll of film and popularizing snapshot photography among the public, and his early advertisements helped turn photography from a serious pastime into a fun-for-the-whole-family hobby.

Although people didn't smile in old photographs, it wasn't necessarily because they were angry. But you couldn't blame them if they were. Can you imagine living your life in black and white?

Q Why is it called rush hour when traffic is the slowest?

A The term "rush hour" was coined in New York around 1890, presumably to describe the frantic pace of life in the city. In today's world, it refers to peak times for traffic. But really, could there be a more blatant misnomer? Let's break it down.

First, you've got the "rush" part. Who's rushing? No one. Because they can't. There are too many cars on the road. Oh, sure, there's the occasional bonehead who's weaving back and forth, changing lanes, and tailgating every car he gets behind, as if his manic behavior is going to somehow make everyone else suddenly, magically speed up. "Rush" in this sense refers not to speed, but to the rush of commuters flooding the transportation system—not just the roads, but also public transportation, where finding a seat can be nearly impossible.

Then you've got the "hour" part. The "hour" in rush hour may be even more misleading than the "rush" part. If you live in anything resembling a large city, you know that this "hour" lasts a heck of a lot longer than sixty minutes. In the morning, the roads can start to get hopelessly clogged by 7:00 AM, and they stay that way until past 9:00 AM. In the evening, you're talking 4:00 PM to 7:00 PM. And that's not counting Fridays, when the afternoon rush starts almost as soon as the morning rush has ended.

No, this is not your traditional chronological hour. This definition of "hour" is one of those secondary classifications—a vague, unmeasured block of time. Not unlike the way it's used in "happy hour," which, come to think of it, is not a bad way to bypass rush-hour frustration altogether.

Q Why do horseshoes bring good luck?

A The horseshoe is like an infomercial product: It's several things rolled into one! No, the horseshoe doesn't slice and dice, but it helps to protect a horse's hoof... it's used in a game called, appropriately enough, horseshoes... and it brings good luck.

Many cultures attribute magical power to the horseshoe—such as the ability to ward off witches, bad fairies, goblins, and other mischievous or evil creatures. So how did this utilitarian hunk of metal develop such a fine reputation?

The horseshoe's crescent shape may have a lot to do with it. From ancient moon worshipers to the Egyptians, the crescent gained a foothold as a potent symbol in mysticism and mythology. The fact that horseshoes are made from iron, which is considered a lucky metal, also has helped. Then there are the horses themselves—horses have often been regarded with awe. Occasionally, as with certain Germanic tribes, horses have even been worshiped as sacred animals. With so much street cred, the horseshoe was destined to be an object of folklore and superstition.

But before you run out hunting for a horseshoe of your own, there are a few luck-related rules you need to know. First, you can't just buy a horseshoe for luck—you have to find it. Second, if there are nails still in it, that's extra lucky—but don't remove them, for gosh sakes; removing them is unlucky. And don't pick up a mule shoe—that's bad luck. The same goes for picking up a broken horseshoe—it has to be whole to be lucky. But if you find a horseshoe that came from the rear hoof of a grey mare, and it has seven nail holes instead of the standard eight, and there are still nails in it—you are totally rocking in luck, dude.

Once you locate a horseshoe, you have a few options to maximize its influence. You can spit on it and make a wish, or you can make a wish and throw it over your left shoulder. But if you aren't into the whole wish-granting thing and you'd rather just have general good luck, you can hang it over a door in your home. Depending on the school of thought you believe, it will either be essential to hang it with the curve up or the curve down. Most people hang it with the prongs up and the curve down; that way, it holds the luck like a bowl and doesn't spill it. But others feel that this keeps the luck from reaching the recipients; these folks go curve-up.

So if you find a horseshoe and you can remember these myriad rules and regulations, perhaps you'll be the luckier for it.

Q Why do old newspapers turn yellow?

A The daily newspaper is an amazing achievement of labor and technology that we sometimes take for granted. It has been said that any one issue of the Sunday *New York Times* contains more information than an educated person in the eighteenth century consumed in a lifetime.

You probably wouldn't want to try to make it through the Sunday *Times* during your morning commute, but this gives you some idea of just how much information even your garden variety daily newspaper offers. And what do you pay for the daily delivery of such a wealth of knowledge? Somewhere in the neighborhood of seventy-five cents per issue. Not a bad deal.

In order to bring you all that content—international reports, the latest from Washington, crime news, arts reviews, horoscopes, sports scores and stats, and that columnist who irritates you so much but whose articles you never fail to read—publishers need to keep costs in line. That's why newsprint is used: It's cheap.

Like all paper, newsprint is made from wood, which is composed primarily of cellulose, hemicellulose, and lignin. Cellulose, which is kind of like the flesh of a tree, is white. Lignin serves as a tree's bones, giving it strength and stability. Even though lignin is strong, it deteriorates with exposure to oxygen. Consequently, paper with lignin in it becomes yellow and brittle over time.

When high-quality paper is manufactured, the lignin is removed. To produce newsprint as cheaply as possible, the manufacturer skips the lignin-removal process. This leaves newsprint especially vulnerable to the elements, so it deteriorates more quickly than more luxurious paper stock. The best way to save newspaper articles is to make laser copies of them on high-quality paper that will last for years without becoming yellow or brittle.

Or, if you're cheap, you can keep the original newsprint and slow the deterioration process by keeping it protected from light and oxygen. In this case, if you want to admire your collection of historic news, you'll need to master the art of reading in the dark while holding your breath.

Q: Why do computers crash?

A: Since they always seem to crash just after you've completed an unparalleled masterpiece, the evidence suggests that some sort of standard evil chip must be installed at the factory. But search as we may, we haven't been able to find it.

Your computer is a complex combination of hardware—machinery like the hard drive, motherboard, and graphics card—and software programs. Like any other machine, your computer hardware can break due to wear and tear. But most crashes have nothing to do with problems related to the physical hardware; they're the results of the software trying to do things that it shouldn't.

A computer program is essentially an incredibly long and complex list of interconnected instructions. If there's a bug in the program, the computer will try to accomplish something that's impossible. This can send a program into an infinite loop—it works on that task and won't do anything else—or it might break the chain of instructions, terminating the program before you've had a chance to save your work.

When a bug causes problems within a particular program, you can usually quit the program and restart the computer. But a computer can freeze up entirely if the software problem causes the operating system to get stuck. The operating system is the software that manages everything you do on your computer—for most people, it's either Microsoft Windows or Mac OS. When you're surfing the Internet while typing a shopping list and listening to some cool music, your operating system is allocating hardware resources to your Web browser, word processor, and music player. Think of it as a middleman: The individual programs send requests to the operating system, and the operating system makes the computer hardware do what it needs to do to carry out these requests.

So how does your operating system freeze up? In one common scenario, two processes can get stuck waiting to hear back from each other. For example, let's say that Process A expects a response from Process B before moving on to any other task; meanwhile, Process B is waiting for information from Process A before moving on itself. If either process is necessary for your operating system to function, the computer can freeze up entirely.

An operating system may also shut down if a program tries to access something for which it doesn't have permission, usually because of a bug. As a safety precaution, the operating system may simply freeze rather than risk an illegal operation that could corrupt the data. It will probably lose whatever is being worked on in the process, though only with the best intentions. That's little consolation, we know.

Q: Why do pregnant women crave pickles?

A: Countless women have successfully brought a baby to term without eating a single pickle, which is one reason why the topic of pregnancy cravings is controversial. No one is exactly sure how many women experience this phenomenon. Some studies say roughly half of pregnant women develop some sort of food craving, while other research puts the number as high as 80 percent. Regardless, the more pertinent question is: Why do some pregnant women get food cravings?

The so-called experts aren't much help. Some physicians attribute these cravings to nothing more than the expectant mother seeking comfort food. A woman, the thinking goes, may attempt to ease the anxiety of pregnancy with such soothing tastes as ice cream or chocolate (which has been shown to stimulate the release of endorphins).

But what about pickles? One research group has postulated that food cravings during pregnancy are the result of a mineral deficiency in a woman's body. Because a mother-to-be's blood volume nearly doubles during pregnancy, it is possible that the nutrient distribution in her bloodstream can become diluted. As a result, a pregnant woman might unconsciously seek out certain foods to restore this balance. If the woman's body is running low on sodium, for example, she might crack open a jar of pickles, which are soaked in a sodium-filled brine.

This theory seems perfectly logical, but there isn't much evidence to back it up. For instance, the American Academy of Pediatrics reports that a lot of kids don't have enough calcium in their diets, but when was the last time you saw a child pass up a soda for a glass of milk?

The most popular theory centers on a factor to which men ascribe to any inexplicable female behavior: raging hormones. It's a fact that the avalanche of hormones released during pregnancy causes a number of discomforts, such as fatigue, swelling, headaches, and mood swings. Does the list sound familiar? It should. It contains the same discomforts many women experience during their "time of the month."

In the second half of the menstrual cycle, the levels of estrogen and progesterone begin to rise, just as they do during pregnancy. Estrogen has been shown to increase the production of the stress hormone cortisol, which raises the body's blood sugar and can lead to cravings for sugary foods. Progesterone is known to raise the body's metabolism and stimulate an appetite for all sorts of foods, including pickles.

But as we said, this is one of many explanations—and they're all inconclusive. Further proof, as if we needed any, that nerds in lab coats don't understand women.

Q: Why does garlic give you bad breath?

A: In Gothic fiction, garlic is powerful enough to scare off vampire princes. In real life, a spicy dinner at Angelo's Ristorante may simply scare off your girlfriend. What makes garlic breath so off-putting?

Garlic, a bulbous perennial plant of the Lily family, is made up of many sulfur-containing compounds. In addition to being responsible for garlic's strong odor, these sulfurous compounds get the blame for the rotten-egg stench of well water and the wholly undeniable funk created by the skunk. At any rate, when you eat garlic, the bacteria that live in your mouth feed on these compounds and proceed to release gases that are filled with their foul fetor. The result? Holy halitosis!

But that's just the half of it. There are really two kinds of garlic breath: primary garlic breath (which strikes right after you munch on a clove) and secondary garlic breath (a relentless, lingering miasma that manifests as the sulfurous compounds in the garlic slowly metabolize and work their way through your bloodstream and get expelled through your lungs).

Says Luke LaBorde, a professor of food science at Penn State University, "The volatile garlic compounds diffuse from the blood to the air deep within the lungs, and we breathe them out." But you know what? It's not only your breath that stinks. Eat enough garlic and those blood-circulating sulfurous compounds will also start to emanate straight from your skin. And they're not Chanel No. 5.

However stinky, garlic does have some redeeming qualities. It is one of the oldest-known medicinal plants, and recent studies suggest that the sulfur-containing compounds that cause bad breath may also work to relax blood vessels, lower blood pressure, and reduce the risk of heart attack. There's even some evidence that garlic may help protect against cancer and fight off the common cold.

Want to reap the benefits of garlic without putting someone's nose out of joint? After eating it, you should brush, floss, gargle with mouthwash, or chomp on some fresh parsley, fennel, or cardamom seeds. And if you're out on a date, just make sure your significant other eats the same garlicky fare as you; simultaneous garlic breath seems to cancel out the otherwise objectionable effects. "You probably don't notice the smell because your olfactory system is saturated and your brain no longer receives 'garlic signals,'" says LaBorde. "It's the same as if you worked in a horse barn: After a while you don't notice the smell."

Q: Why do so many country names end in "-stan"?

A: No, there was no Stan the Conqueror running around founding countries in ancient times. The real answer is a lot less exciting. There are "-stan" countries for the same reason there are "-land" countries—*stan* is an old Persian word meaning "place," "land," or "home." As people from ancient Persia (modern-day Iran) spread to different areas of western Asia, they took the suffix with them.

Today, there are seven independent "-stan" nations in central Asia (including some that creep over into Eastern Europe); five are former republics of the Soviet Union. There are also three "-stan" republics in the Russian Federation, three "-stan" provinces in Iran, and several historical "-stan" regions in various Asian countries.

Typically, place names formed with "-stan" describe a land in terms of its inhabitants. For example, Afghanistan means "land of the Afghans." In other cases, "-stan" formations evoke the landscape itself, like the name Dagestan (a Russian republic), which means "land of the mountains."

Pakistan is a recent addition to the "-stan" list. In 1930, the Muslim philosopher Sir Muhammad Iqbal called for a new Muslim state to be carved out of what was then British India. Students who supported the idea proposed calling the new country Pakistan for its double meaning. It literally meant "land of the pure" (*pak*), and according to Peter Blood's book *Pakistan: A Country Study*, it also incorporated letters from some of the predominantly Muslim regions in the area—**P**unjab, **A**fghania, **K**ashmir, **I**ran, **S**indh, **T**ukharistan, **A**fghanistan, and Balochista**n**.

So, here's an interesting thought for you: If Persians had discovered the New World, we might all be living in the United States of Americastan.

Q **Why is everything more painful when it's cold?**

A Ever tried to catch a football on a frigid November day? You might have noticed that the slap of the pigskin against your palms had a sting that it didn't have in August. Did you suddenly become some kind of mama's boy? No—it actually does hurt more when it's cold.

When we're cold, our bodies' pain sensors become more sensitive. These nerves are integrated with the skin, and extremes in temperature seem to send them into overdrive. This is actually a good thing. Pain is our bodies' way of telling us to stop and pay attention to what's wrong. In this case, pain is saying: "Hey, fool, you're looking at some serious injury. Quit tossing around the pigskin and go have a cup of hot cocoa."

This response occurs when it's frigid because our bodies are more susceptible to injury when they're cold. For example, cold muscles will contract to produce warmth—head out the door on a nippy morn and you can almost feel your body drawing in on itself.

When muscles contract like this, they become more rigid and less flexible, which means that they are much harder to stretch and a lot easier to pull or injure. If you're a football fan, you know that it's not unusual for a player to be carted off the snowy field clutching at a strained muscle or twisted joint during a late-season game.

People who suffer from arthritis will tell you that cold temperatures are downright chilling to bones, too. Dr. Randall L. Braddom, a physiatrist and specialist in physical medicine and rehabilitation at Riverview Medical Center in New Jersey, says that cold temps can cause the circulatory system to conserve warm blood around the heart, which results in less blood being sent to the extremities. As a result, joints become stiffer and people experience more pain.

Weather-related pain might also be connected to barometric pressure. Have you heard someone say his or her bum knee aches before it snows or rains? Dr. Braddom says that drops in air pressure might cause inflamed tissues in and around joints to expand, thereby bringing on the big hurt.

What can be done to alleviate cold-weather pain? We all know that there's no controlling Mother Nature, so you really just have to adapt—pop your favorite anti-inflammatory pill and wear multiple layers of clothing. Better yet, pack up your belongings and move to Arizona.

Q: Why is a football shaped that way?

A: Would you rather call it a bladder? Because that's what footballs were made of before mass-produced rubber or leather balls became the norm.

The origins of the ball and the game can be traced to the ancient Greeks, who played something called harpaston. As in football, players scored by kicking, passing, or running over the opposition's goal line. The ball in harpaston was often made of a pig's bladder. This is because pigs' bladders were easy to find, roundish in shape, relatively simple to inflate and seal, and fairly durable. (If you think playing ball with an internal organ is gross, consider what the pig's bladder replaced: a human head.)

Harpaston evolved into European rugby, which evolved into American football. By the time the first "official" football game was played at Rutgers University in New Jersey in the fall of 1869, the ball had evolved, too. To make the ball more durable and consistently shaped, it was covered with a protective layer that was usually made of leather.

Still, the extra protection didn't help the pig's bladder stay permanently inflated, and there was a continuous need to reinflate the ball. Whenever play was stopped, the referee unlocked the ball—yes, there was a little lock on it to help keep it inflated—and a player would pump it up.

Footballs back then were meant to be round, but the sphere was imperfect for a couple reasons. First, the bladder lent itself more to an oval shape; even the most perfectly stitched leather covering couldn't force the bladder to remain circular. Second, as a game wore on, players got tired and were less enthused about reinflating the ball. As a result, the ball would flatten out and take on more of an oblong shape. The ball was easier to grip in that shape, and the form slowly gained popularity, particularly after the forward pass was introduced in 1906.

Through a series of rule changes relating to its shape, the football became slimmer and ultimately developed its current look. And although it's been many decades since pigs' bladders were relieved of their duties, the football's nickname—a "pigskin"—lives on.

Q: Why aren't all gas caps on the same side of the car?

A: Your uncle's 1956 Chevy hid it behind the left taillight. On your dad's '65 Mustang, it was above the back license plate and beneath the galloping-horse emblem. Today's BMW has it on the right rear fender. Drive a Honda? Check the left rear fender. Own a Ford? It's on the right. Unless it's a Ford Fusion; then it's on the left.

We're talking gas caps, and they are no longer at the very back of the car because the fuel tank is no longer at the very back of the car. It's in front of the rear axle, protected from harm in a crash, and its filler neck enters from the side. But why isn't it on the same side from car to car?

Some speculate that it's always opposite the exhaust pipe to prevent fires from dribbled gas. Not true, say automotive designers; some cars, after all, have exhaust outlets on both sides. Another notion suggests that caps face the shoulder of the road so that luckless motorists needn't stand in traffic to refill a car that's run out of gas.

But some cars from countries that drive on the right side of the road, like the United States, have left-side caps. And some cars from left-side-drive countries, like Japan and England, have right-side caps. A few optimistic souls even believe that automakers alternate sides so that we don't all queue up in the same line at the gas pump. They're mistaken.

For its part, the National Highway Traffic Safety Administration doesn't care which side the cap's on, as long as the car meets standards designed to reduce deaths and injuries from fires caused by fuel spillage during and after crashes. Tests set precise limits on the volume of fuel that can be spilled during rollovers and in rear impacts at specific rates of speed.

How automakers satisfy the requirements is their own affair. Once designers have a tank and filler neck that meet the standards, something they call "packaging" determines on which side the cap goes. Designers must route the filler neck around the suspension and exhaust components, trunk cavity, wheel housings, and door cutouts—all the stuff in the tail of a modern automobile.

Some manufacturers, like BMW and Honda, engineer all of their cars to standardize the cap on the same side. Others, like Ford and General Motors, follow the packaging dictates of each individual car. Some of today's fuel gauges display a little arrow telling us which side the cap is on. Sure, it's nice, but it's no galloping horse.

Q: Why do cows lie down before it rains?

A: It's a common bit of folklore: If a bunch of cows are lying down, it means that rain is coming. Scientists have even examined this phenomenon, and they've come up with a couple of theories:

- Cows sense the moisture in the air and lie down in order to preserve heat before the rain comes.
- Cows lie down while the ground is still dry so that they won't have to wallow in the mud.

In reality, cows lie down for one reason and one reason only: to relax. They will remain standing until they feel the need to relax, and then they will take a seat. Other factors might influence their shift into relaxation mode—maybe it's hot, maybe the cattle are a bit tired or stiff—but the goal remains the same.

Animals have been known to dabble in weather predictions. Cats and dogs are thought to be able to predict earthquakes, and folks in Alaska look to animals to gauge how severe the winter will be. Animals are generally thought to be more sensitive to changes in the atmosphere than we humans are, so we learn to read their reactions in order to see what's ahead.

But in this case, we're looking for something that isn't even there. A common dairy cow will spend 60 percent of its life lying down. Chances are, at some point in the day, every cow on the range will be resting on its laurels, taking a midday siesta. So before deciding whether you need an umbrella, don't look at a cow pasture. Instead, check The Weather Channel.

Q Why do old churches have steeples?

A Because they are pointing to heaven. Other reasons have been offered over the years, but clergymen and historians generally agree that steeples atop churches are meant to guide a person's gaze skyward.

Religious buildings have led the eyes heavenward for millennia. Egyptians had their obelisks, for example. It could be argued that these structures are phallic symbols, but the practical fact is that towers and pinnacles make temples and other religious buildings easy to see. And they fill believers with awe.

As far back as the Dark Ages, watchtowers were features of churches, which were often the biggest buildings in town. Documentation is hard to come by, but at some point the towers began to serve less as perches for watchmen and more as cubbies from which to hang bells and as mounts for crosses that could be seen for miles. Architects began adding purely decorative spires to Christian churches in the twelfth century, when Gothic architecture was all the rage.

The wooden steeple as we know it today came into vogue later. On September 2, 1666, a fire destroyed much of London. Thirteen thousand homes were incinerated, along with more than eighty churches. King Charles II commissioned Christopher Wren, considered one of England's greatest architects, to rebuild St. Paul's Cathedral and about fifty other churches.

Wren topped one of his first projects, St. Mary-le-Bow, with a steeple, and Londoners were duly inspired. The city was soon filled with steeple-topped churches, and colonists carried the architectural style to America.

Steeples are no longer church staples everywhere in the United States—the custom is disappearing in California and other western states. In the South, however, most congregations wouldn't think of building a church without a steeple. A steeple continues to be excellent housing for a church bell—and in these modern days, it is just as likely to be a hiding place for microwave antennas for cell phones.

Q: Why do dogs lick people?

A: When a dog licks your face, it feels kind of like you're being kissed. And according to the most popular theory related to dog licking, that perception isn't far from the truth.

One reason dogs lick is to show affection. Like a kiss hello between two good friends, a few licks on the hand or the face express how the canine feels about the person in its life. Just like we humans, some dogs are more affectionate than others. A dog's personality and age can influence how openly it licks—an excitable young pup is apt to be more forthcoming with its affection than a stately older dog. Dog experts say that licking is basically a social activity. For example, puppies lick each other as displays of affection and to groom each other; they'll lick their mothers to indicate that they're ready to feed.

So a dog's tongue on your skin can mean a couple of things: Fido might want some love, or some food. If those licks turn to nibbles, you'll know that it's the latter.

Q: Why is it harder to lose weight as you age?

A: As the years pass and the birthdays mount, we watch in horror as our sinewy bodies become blobs. Is there any way to halt this grotesque march into oblivion? Not really. The main problem is that we tend to lose muscle mass as we get older—even if our caloric intake is modest, less muscle leads to a slower metabolism and a greater propensity to pack on unwanted pounds.

A pound of muscle burns about thirty-five to fifty calories per day; a pound of fat burns around three calories per day. Do the math, and you'll see that it doesn't add up in your favor: Even when we're not doing something strenuous, muscle will burn about twelve to seventeen times more calories than will body fat. In other words, with greater muscle mass, we have a much faster metabolism and can consume more calories before we start putting on weight. But if the ratio of fat to muscle tips to the blubbery side of things, the pounds add up.

After age 40, we typically lose about 1 percent of our lean muscle mass per year. Part of this is the natural result of the aging process: As we get older, the body produces less testosterone and human growth hormone, the two primary hormones that control muscle growth. But our daily habits can also be significant factors. Think about it: The routine of a twenty-year-old involves a lot more physical activity than that of someone who's thirty or older. Compare walking across campus several times to sitting at a desk for eight hours and then trudging home to sit on the couch and watch television. A sedentary lifestyle leads to less muscle mass.

Many people exacerbate the problem by going on extreme diets or skipping meals. If we cut too far back on calories or go, say, sixteen hours without eating, we can slow down our metabolisms. And when food intake dips too precipitously, the body switches into "starvation mode" and starts storing more calories as fat.

This "starvation mode" made sense when we were cavemen: Lean times could be a sign of even leaner times to come, and saving up energy was a necessary precaution. But today, lean times can lead to a ballooning stomach. Intense dieting actually makes weight loss more difficult to sustain because the body adapts to a lack of food and burns fewer calories.

A balanced approach is your best bet. Consume a doctor-recommended number of calories throughout the day and expend energy through cardiovascular exercise and strength training. If you build up enough muscle mass, you can boost your metabolism, push back Father Time a bit, and reclaim some of the glory of your college years.

Q Why can't the government just print more money to stimulate the economy?

A For some insight into this fascinating question, let's travel to Zimbabwe. As Zimbabwe's economic health began to worsen in the 1990s, President Robert Mugabe ordered the printing of more money to meet government expenses. Once among Africa's richest nations, Zimbabwe was in economic shambles by 2008; the country's rate of inflation had soared to 2.2 million percent.

Inflation pushed prices so high that the Zimbabwean government started printing currency in outlandish denominations. A ten-million-dollar bill that was released in January 2008 was soon followed by a fifty-billion-dollar bill. Upon the release of a hundred-billion-dollar bill, a Zimbabwean man told the British Broadcasting Corporation, "Nowadays, for my expenses a day, I need about [five hundred billion dollars]. So [one hundred billion dollars] can't do anything because for me to go home I need $250 billion, so this [note] is worthless." The man was talking about bus fare. Trust us, you don't want to know how much it cost to buy food for a week.

The truth is, a government can print more money to stimulate its economy, and sometimes it works. In the United States, when the economy gets a little shaky, the Federal Reserve prints more money and uses it to buy bonds from banks. With extra cash on hand, banks can loan more money to individuals and businesses; this stimulates the economy.

But this requires judicious handling. If the U.S. government simply began to print wads of cash and hand it out to all of us, we would have more money to spend on goods. It seems likely that we would flock to malls and grocery stores en masse and buy stuff like crazy. Demand for goods would soar, and to cope with this new demand, manufacturers would have two choices:

1) Produce more. How do you increase production? Buy more equipment, pay production workers for more hours, and purchase more of the materials necessary to produce your goods. All of this would increase the cost of production, and to cover that increase, the prices of the goods would have to be raised.

2) Take the pressure off by lowering demand. How do you lower demand? Artificially raise prices.

Either way, more money in the system would cause prices to increase. That's inflation, and the danger is that money would become essentially worthless. We never want to see guys hanging around the bus stop asking, "Brother, can you spare five hundred billion dollars?"

Q: Why do firehouses keep Dalmatians?

A: A great debate rages over whether the Dalmatian hails from Egypt, Asia, or Dalmatia (which is a region in Eastern Europe that is largely situated in Croatia), for which the dog is named. Luckily, we don't have to answer that question. We've been charged with telling you how Dalmatians wound up in firehouses, which is a comparatively easy assignment.

Dalmatians are hardworking, sensitive, and fiercely loyal dogs that have great memories and a passion for running and hunting vermin. They're also quite social—they become lonely and depressed without regular interaction. In addition to forming strong bonds with their human owners, they get along famously with horses, on which they have a calming effect.

Based on these traits, Dalmatians were trained and used in England, Scotland, and Wales as "coach dogs" by the seventeen hundreds. The horse-drawn carriage was the main mode of transport at the time, and the coach dog ran under or beside the carriage, occasionally speeding ahead to clear other dogs or people out the way for the horses. Furthermore, Dalmatians guarded the carriage and horses when the master was away. In an age when horse thievery was common, a stagecoach driver with a Dalmatian could afford the luxury of sleeping in a hotel room rather than with the coach and horses, since he knew that his trusty dog would sound its *woof-woof* alarm if anyone disturbed the carriage.

Fire departments of this era also relied on horses to pull their specially equipped wagons. Enter Dalmatians, which cleared traffic as the wagons sped to a fire. Once there, the dogs kept the horses calm and the equipment safe while the firefighters did their jobs.

Dalmatians performed their duties equally well at American firehouses, but their gig ended when engine-powered fire trucks rolled onto the scene in the first part of the twentieth century. Now Dalmatians are relegated to the role of mascot in fire departments in England, the United States, and Canada—a symbolic nod to the rough-hewn days when blazes weren't fought without them.

Q Why do mattresses come with tags that say, "Do Not Remove Under Penalty of Law"?

A The controversy has raged for years. It has pitted neighbor against neighbor, brother against brother, American against American. You've heard the arguments and seen the bumper stickers: IF REMOVING MATTRESS TAGS IS A CRIME, ONLY CRIMINALS WILL HAVE MATTRESSES WITHOUT TAGS and THEY CAN HAVE MY MATTRESS TAG—WHEN THEY PRY IT FROM MY COLD, DEAD HANDS!

What's the big deal with mattress tags? Like many of the edicts that shape our consumer culture, the law that prohibits the removal of mattress tags can be traced to good old-fashioned entrepreneurship in the late nineteenth and early twentieth centuries.

It seems that some enterprising mattress makers of the era might have sold a few mattresses that were stuffed with straw, rags, horsehair, or worse, and didn't bother to mention it to their customers. Hey, what's a little lice among friends? So to ensure that folks could be certain the bedding they were buying really was made out of what the manufacturer said it was, mattress makers were required by law to affix labels listing the materials that were used. But here's something you can do if you've got a naughty side: Tear off the tag. Rip that sucker off! You can do it. Know why? There's a loophole in the law: Nobody can legally remove the tag... except the consumer.

Q Why is the pirate flag called a Jolly Roger?

A With the 1883 publication of Robert Louis Stevenson's *Treasure Island*, the popular idea of the pirate germinated: a witty rogue with an eye patch, a peg-leg, and a smart-ass parrot, sailing the seven seas under the Jolly Roger, good-naturedly plundering booty and instigating a little plank-walking. Unfortunately for those romantics who long for the swashbuckling days of yore, most of Bob Lou Steve's details aren't particularly accurate.

There is little evidence that something as dramatic as "walking the plank" happened much, and parrots were rarely recorded as ships' mascots. But calling the pirate flag the "Jolly Roger" was one of the details Stevenson got right.

For hundreds of years, ships have hoisted the colors of their home country to let other ships know from where they hail. In the golden age of piracy, pirates used this form of communication as well, though more deviously. Often, pirates would fly flags of certain countries as a form of deception, in order to get close to their prey. Once they were within striking distance, the buccaneers would lower their false flags and raise their own ensigns. These flags varied from pirate to pirate, but they all meant the same thing: "Surrender, hand over your booty, and we will not kill you." Though if the pirates raised a red flag, it meant, "We will kill you and take your booty." (One might say these flags were the original "booty call.")

French pirates most prominently used the red flag as a symbol of imminent death, and among these pirates, such a flag became known as a *joli rouge* ("pretty red"). The English, hewing to their long tradition of making no effort to correctly pronounce foreign words, turned this into the "Jolly Roger."

Another theory points to a legendary Tamil pirate by the name of Ali Raja. Raja ruled the Indian Ocean and had such a reputation that even English seamen had heard of the pirate captain. It's not hard to imagine how Europeans who were unfamiliar with Middle Eastern languages might corrupt "Ali Raja" into "Jolly Roger."

The least interesting hypothesis points to the fact that in England during piracy's glory days, the devil was often referred to as "Old Roger." That, combined with the grinning appearance of the skull symbol, led to the flag being called the "Jolly Roger." Unfortunately, there is no definitive evidence that supports one theory over another.

The origin of the familiar skull-and-crossbones image is also unclear. The image had been used as a general symbol of death long before pirates appropriated it—crusaders used the symbol in the 1100s, for example. The first recorded use of the skull-and-crossbones on a pirate flag was in 1700, when a French buccaneer named Emmanuel Wynne hoisted it. After that, the black flag with a variation of the image appeared more frequently and sometimes included hourglasses, spears, and dancing skeletons.

Once Stevenson published *Treasure Island*, the skull-and-crossbones—along with the mythical parrot—became forever associated with pirates in the popular mind. The novel is also famous for introducing the phrase, "Yo, ho, ho, and a bottle of rum" into pirate lore. We don't know what that means, either.

Q Why do mosquitoes bite some people more than others?

A Mosquitoes are attracted to some people for the same reason that some folks are attracted to bakeries early in the morning: The goods smell delicious.

One theory suggests that mosquitoes are picky eaters that choose potential victims based on blood type. Eighty-five percent of humans secrete a chemical marker through their pores that indicates their blood type. In some cases, the marker hits the mosquito the same way the smell of fresh-baked bread hits human nostrils. Microscopic drops of saliva form around the insect's proboscis, the little devil hits the smorgasbord, and it digs in as soon as it feels safe.

A study conducted in 2004 showed that mosquitoes land on individuals with Type O blood more often than they feast on those with any other blood type. Conversely, Type A appears to be the least popular flavor for mosquitoes. The fortunate 15 percent of humanity whose pores do not secrete a blood-type marker suffer the fewest bites; like a roadside diner with a burned-out neon sign, they attract hardly any customers at all.

In 2006, scientists performed a test using a Y-shaped tube. Two individuals stuck a hand in the tube, and mosquitoes that were released into the tube could choose which hand to bite. Scientists collected perspiration from the person who attracted the fewest mosquitoes to study its chemical makeup. Researchers also believe that some people may emit a masking odor that actually repels mosquitoes. By studying the chemicals these lucky people excrete, scientists hope to create a more potent, less irritating insect repellent.

Pregnant women might be particularly interested in such a breakthrough. Mosquitoes are attracted to carbon dioxide, and pregnant women exhale more carbon dioxide than the average person. Furthermore, a pregnant belly is a bit warmer than a normal belly, which may also appeal to mosquitoes.

Alcohol consumption has also been shown to increase the likelihood of bites. This may be because of a change in the blood's chemical makeup when it is processing a few drinks, and because of the rise in body temperature that comes with consuming too much alcohol.

Want to avoid mosquito bites? Stay away from alcohol, don't go outside if you are pregnant, and pray that you are among the lucky 15 percent of the population that doesn't secrete blood-type markers. If nothing else, hope others in your party have their neon lights flashing "Type O!"

Q: Why do golfers hate to putt?

A: Most golfers hate to putt, at some level. Sometimes at a very visible, sweaty level. Even though golfers know it's possible to mess up every single shot from tee to green, putting is what winds up freaking them out.

Why? The easy answer is that putting is hard. Even for the pros. "I play along every year waiting for one week, maybe two, when I can putt," says Larry Nelson. And Nelson has been one of the best putters in professional golf for almost three decades.

We amateurs tend to think that pros make almost all of their putts. In fact, they miss at least six out of every hundred from two feet—an astonishingly high number. They make no more than one in every six putts from twenty feet. All we do is make things worse by imagining it's easier for the pros than it is.

And this gets us closer to the heart of the matter. Golfers tend to think too much, especially on the green.

"*Happy Gilmore* is a pretty good instructional film," says PGA teaching pro Peter Donahue. He explains that the loopy Adam Sandler character has the most vital trait in a good putter: He's happy to putt. "Golfers train themselves not to love to shoot but to be afraid to miss," Donahue says. "It's like Red Auerbach said in basketball: 'I don't care if you miss, just don't be afraid to shoot.'"

The best putters in the world are touring and teaching pros, obviously. But the next best, according to Donahue, are beginners. Why? It goes back to that thinking thing. Beginners don't ponder—they just putt.

After searching far and wide, we did uncover at least one person who likes to putt: PGA golfer Ben Crenshaw. "From the very beginning I enjoyed putting," he says in his autobiography. "I loved putting because it was just plain fun, and it fascinated me to watch the ball roll over those blades of grass."

Crenshaw, of course, is in the minority. Take it from Larry Eimers, a sports psychologist from Durham, North Carolina, who has counseled many a tortured putter: "You're in a risk area where you're liable to suffer humiliation or embarrassment if you miss it.... Everyone hates [the short] putt, because if you make it, no one gives a damn, but if you miss it, everyone raises their eyebrows. In the end, you're working eighteen holes to avoid humiliation."

Did we mention that golfers hate to putt?

Q: Why don't penguins and polar bears get frostbite?

A: If you spent an afternoon strolling around barefoot at the North Pole or the South Pole, your feet would freeze and—best-case scenario—you'd end the day short a couple of toes. But polar bears and penguins obviously don't wear boots, and they seem to be fine. What's the deal?

Scientists tell us that the human body evolved to its present state on the toasty African plains, where ice and subzero temperatures are barely imaginable. It's no surprise, then, that your body can't function without significant protection in arctic conditions. When your extremities—your feet and hands—get very cold, your body does something that may seem counterintuitive. As an act of self-preservation, it lets your extremities get colder, constricting the blood vessels that feed those parts in order to conserve heat for the rest of the body.

This helps maintain your core temperature in frigid weather, but it wreaks havoc on your hands and feet. The eventual result is frostbite—the tissue dies off. It can also lead to hypothermia, a dangerous drop in overall body temperature, even if the rest of your body is bundled up.

Polar bears don't have this problem because their feet are like natural boots. Their huge paws come equipped with thick pads on the bottom and heavy fur on top. This thick insulation keeps their paws from losing heat rapidly, so there's no need for the bear's body to cut off the blood flow.

The furry, padded-feet approach wouldn't work so well for penguins. For one thing, they need relatively unencumbered feet so that they can swim quickly. Perhaps more importantly, since they're covered in feathers and insulated by layers of fat, their feet are their only means for releasing excess heat when they exert a lot of energy. As a result, penguins evolved highly efficient self-warming feet.

As in humans, the flow of blood to penguins' feet is controlled in order to regulate overall temperature loss. But the blood vessels in their feet are arranged differently than those of humans: The vessels that carry warm blood into the feet are located close to the vessels that take cold blood out of the feet. The warm blood heats up the cold blood that's flowing back into the torso, which prevents their overall body temperature from plummeting. What's more, their bodies are calibrated to keep their feet just a degree or two above freezing; this wards off frostbite.

Penguins have another trick to keep their feet warm. When it gets really cold, a penguin might rest on its heels and tail to keep the majority of its footpads off the ice. As for you? We recommend insulated boots.

Q: Why does an orchestra conductor need a baton?

A. So there was this seventeenth-century composer named Jean-Baptiste Lully who was conducting his beautiful music at a rehearsal. As always, he was keeping time with a huge wooden staff that he pounded on the floor. On this fateful day, however, Lully missed the floor and drove the staff right into his foot.

No, this is not the moment the conductor's baton was born. Lully did not have an epiphany and say, "You know, I should use something smaller to direct my music." Nevertheless, the moment remains part of music history. An abscess developed on Lully's right foot that turned to gangrene. The composer did not have the foot amputated, causing the gangrene to spread and eventually leading to his death. There you have it—a conducting fatality!

So when did conductors trade in those clumsy, and potentially lethal, wooden staffs for the symbolically powerful batons? And do they really need them? Don't a conductor's hands contain ten God-made batons?

Some conductors today use their hands and fingers, but most have a baton that they move to the music. The theory is that the baton—usually ten to twenty-four inches long and made of wood, fiberglass, or carbon—magnifies a conductor's patterns and gestures, making them clearer for the orchestra or ensemble.

Orchestras date to the late sixteenth century during the Baroque period, and conductors back then used the same type of staff that felled Lully. Sometimes there was no conductor at all. Instead, the leader was most often a keyboardist, who would guide the orchestra when his hands were free, or a violinist, who would set the tempo and give directions by beating the neck of his instrument or making other movements. At other times, the keyboardist or violinist simply played louder so the rest of the orchestra could follow his lead.

As written music grew more complex, orchestras needed more direction than a keyboardist or violinist could provide. Conductors started appearing in France in the eighteenth century and emerged in earnest early in the nineteenth century. Still, there was no baton—rolled up paper was the tool of choice.

German composer, violinist, and conductor Louis Spohr claimed to have introduced the formal baton to the music world in a performance in 1820, but that simply might have been boastfulness. It is widely thought that he only used a baton in rehearsals.

It's possible that German composer, pianist, and conductor Felix Mendelssohn was the first to use an actual baton in a performance. According to *The Cambridge Companion to Conducting*, Mendelssohn used a baton in 1829 and again in 1832 with the Philharmonic Society of London. The next year, a baton was used regularly with the Philharmonic—and today, almost every conductor wields one.

Even though the baton is a lot safer than the wooden staff, there have been some accidents along the way. For example, German conductor Daniel Turk's motions became so animated during a performance in 1810 that he hit a chandelier above his head and was showered with glass. What is it with these guys?

There was more baton craziness in 2006 and 2007. First, the conductor of the Harvard University band set a record by using a baton that was ten-and-a-half or twelve-and-a-half feet long, depending on whom you listen to. The next year, the University of Pennsylvania band claimed to have bested that record with its fifteen-foot, nine-inch baton. There were no reports of a Lully moment on either occasion.

Q: Why do we give names to hurricanes and cyclones?

A: Every year, as summer fades to fall, the news reports start: Teddy is wreaking havoc in the Caribbean; Bertha is causing trouble on the Eastern seaboard. We conjure images of shrill-voiced vacationers in straw hats, noses thick with sun block, making life miserable for restaurant servers and hotel clerks. But while Teddy and Bertha may sound like a nasty couple, they are, in fact, tropical storms.

Beyond anthropomorphizing storms, naming them has a practical application. There may be several storms brewing in the same region of the world at once. At one time, these storms were identified by their latitudinal and longitudinal coordinates. But that was clumsy and could result in miscommunication between forecasters and the public. Assigning storms short, distinct names is more effective.

The custom of naming storms has a long history. In the nineteenth century, hurricanes in the West Indies were named for the saint's day on which they arrived. During World War II, meteorologists in the American armed forces assigned women's names to storms, reportedly using the monikers of their wives and girlfriends for inspiration.

In 1953—following a brief period during which storm names were drawn from the phonetic alphabet (Able, Baker, Charlie, and so forth)—forecasters in the United States revived the World War II custom of using women's names. The World Meteorological Organization has since assumed the coordination of the process in order to ensure international consistency. In the spirit of gender equality, storm names began to alternate between male and female in 1979.

Today, tropical storms are named using rotating six-year lists. Each part of the world that is prone to tropical storms is assigned its own set of lists. The naming is done alphabetically: The year's first storm begins with A, the second with B, and so forth. Meanwhile, the name of a particularly deadly or damaging storm is retired from the list.

If by chance you're a Quentin, Ursula, Xavier, Yuri, or Zubin, and you desire meteorological immortality, you had best attain it by becoming a famous TV weather forecaster. Why? So few names begin with Q, U, X, Y, and Z that these letters are excluded from the storm list.

Q: Why are three straight bowling strikes called a Turkey?

A: We love bowling—and why not? We love the mustaches, the tinted glasses, the fingerless gloves. We love that air-vent thingy on the ball rack, and we love the swirling balls that are inscribed with names like Lefty and Dale. We love the satin shirts and the multi-colored shoes (okay, maybe not the shoes so much).

But what we love most are the terms. The Dutch 200, the Brooklyn strike, the Cincinnati, the Jersey, the Greek Church, and especially the Turkey. We have no idea what any of these terms mean, but we love them all the same.

Believe it or not, bowling wasn't always the sexy, hip sport played by highly trained athletes that it is today. Some historians trace bowling's roots back to 3200 BC, while others place its origin in Europe in the third century AD. Regardless, some form of bowling has been popular for centuries.

For much of this history, however, bowling didn't have a particularly sterling reputation. Quite the opposite: Legend has it that King Edward III banned bowling after his good-for-nothing soldiers kept skipping archery practice to roll. And well into the nineteenth century, American towns were outlawing bowling, largely because of the gambling that went along with it.

Despite these attempts at suppression—or perhaps because of them—bowling increased in popularity. In 1895, the American Bowling Congress (which is now known as the United States Bowling Congress) was formed, and local and regional bowling clubs began proliferating. It was around this time that the term "Turkey," which signifies three strikes in a row, arrived on the scene.

In an attempt to cash in on the burgeoning popularity of the newly sanctioned sport, as well as draw customers, many bowling alley proprietors offered a free live turkey to bowlers who successfully rolled three strikes in a row during Thanksgiving or Christmas week. Sadly, turkeys are no longer awarded at bowling alleys, although the tradition of shouting "Turkey" when somebody manages three strikes in a row continues.

So the next time you cry "fowl" at the bowling alley, you can take pride in knowing that you're continuing a time-honored tradition. Now if we could just figure out who decided two-toned bowling shoes were a good idea, we'd really be on to something.

Q: Why do fruits and vegetables change colors as they ripen?

A: Brilliant color is one way to tell if your bananas, apples, tomatoes, and berries are sweet, juicy, and ready to eat. Ever bite into a green banana? That's bitter, brother!

How and why do fruits and vegetables change color? Well, you know how every autumn the leaves turn from green to rich shades of yellow, red, and brown? Aging—or ripening—fruits and vegetables go through a similar process.

Most unripe fruits and veggies are hard, sour, and—you guessed it—green. That green color is largely due to the presence of chlorophyll. (Quick flashback to science class: That's the green pigment found in all green plants. It's vital for photosynthesis, which allows plants to get energy from sunlight.) As growing fruits and vegetables mature, rising levels of acid and enzymes cause the green chlorophyll pigments to break down. That's when your produce begins to show its true hues.

Bananas and certain varieties of apples have vivid skins of yellow and red, respectively, waiting to emerge from underneath that green layer of chlorophyll. Other fruits, like tomatoes, make brand-new color compounds (in their case, glossy red-orange ones) as their chlorophyll begins to wane.

As for peppers, their final coloration depends on their degree of ripeness. No, those aren't different varieties of bell peppers at the grocery store—it just so happens that peppers are vegetables that are good to eat at any stage. They change from green (unripe) to yellow and orange (semi-ripe) to red (fully ripe). That's why green peppers are slightly bitter, while the red ones taste sweet.

What does this all have to do with the autumn leaves? The changing colors of falling leaves and ripening fruits and vegetables is simply a sign of plant senescence (a fancy term biologists use to describe the natural process of deterioration with age). The brilliant tints that are found on ripe fruit and vegetable peels are comprised of active and healthy antioxidants. Eat some every day—preferably before they turn brown and mushy.

Q **Why do newer car models have letters and numbers instead of names?**

A Goodbye, Lincoln Continental; hello, Lincoln MKS. So long, Cadillac Eldorado; hi there, Cadillac XLR. *Adios*, Acura Legend; *hola*, Acura RL.

What is going on? Why are automakers veering from perfectly good names and toward a jumble of letters and numbers? What exactly is an xB? Or an S34? Where's the Thunderbird when you need it? As it turns out, image enhancement, brand building, and a shortage of great car names are all responsible for this gibberish.

Image is just about everything to an upscale car brand. It's no accident that the automakers most associated with non-word names tend to be the upscale varieties, such as BMW (with its 330i and 760iL, for example) and Mercedes-Benz (C350, S550). These old-line automakers have used alphanumerics for years as codes that are clear once you crack them. The E350, for example, belongs to Mercedes-Benz's E-Class line, which slots between the lower-priced C-Class and top-line S-Class lines; 350 denotes its 3.5-liter engine.

Rivals who were hungry to project premium images imitated this convention, but seldom with much meaning behind the letters or numbers. The RL, TL, TSX, MDX, or RDX on the back of an Acura, for instance, doesn't actually stand for anything, the company admits. Acura says it went with letters in order to emphasize the Acura brand and differentiate its luxury cars from the mainstream wares of parent company Honda.

Some automakers choose alphanumerics in order to subjugate individual car models to the lord of brand identity. They insist that an owner who's prompted to say "I drive a Lincoln" or "I drive a Cadillac" instead of "I drive an MKZ" or "I drive an STS" is spreading brand recognition. This thinking leads to such badges as the intentionally obtuse MKS from Lincoln and the meaning-challenged SRX from Cadillac. Skeptics of this logic are legion. And some cynics note how fond moniker-makers are of the letters S, E, and X.

Mustang and Cougar, Firebird and Fury, Electra and Riviera—all evocative, and all taken. After World War II, American car buyers had fifty-five individual models on their shopping lists; today, they have almost three hundred. Car namers find it easier to conjure up letters than to comb a thesaurus. It's less expensive, too, given the cost of research, customer clinics, trademark issues, and global retailing. The use of letters also helps manufacturers steer clear of unwanted meanings. Buick was caught in the act when it learned French-Canadians would associate the term "LaCrosse" not with a new sedan, but with slang for, um, self-gratification. The Canadian LaCrosse became the Allure.

Some automakers still believe in the power of a name. What's more appropriate to gung-ho Jeep than a model called the Patriot? Others gamely invent their own names. Picture Volkswagen's harried naming team, under deadline and out of ideas, relieving late-night tension with a stein or three and becoming convinced that combining "tiger" with "leguan"—the German word for "iguana"—was *wunderbar* for its new SUV. It may not have come about quite that way, but VW dealers are now selling something called the Tiguan.

Q: Why does gin taste like pine needles?

A: Simply put, it's the juniper berry that gives gin its piney fresh flavor. The taste of gin can be traced to this fleshy, scaly, and bitter seed cone, which comes from a shrub that, like the pine tree, is a member of the evergreen family.

The forerunner of gin, a Dutch spirit called *genever*, is said to have originated in Holland sometime in the early seventeenth century as a medicine for stomach ailments. Juniper berries flavored the concoction, and also lent their diuretic and anti-inflammatory qualities to the brew. The British soon stole the idea and began distilling their own version, called gin, which had certain... recreational benefits. Suffice it to say, by the mid-seventeen hundreds, more gin was consumed in England than beer.

Gin's popularity continued to grow, and sometime after the advent of the continuous still in 1831, the English began producing their own distinctive variety: London dry. Today, most of the gin produced around the world falls into the dry category. Dry gin begins with a more neutral base spirit rather than the sugary, malty one first used by the Dutch, so the botanical flavors that are added for the second phase of distilling come through more clearly. Juniper berries remain the most dominant flavoring, but manufacturers have developed formulas that include various combinations and proportions of other herbs and spices, such as angelica root, anise, coriander, caraway, lime, lemon and orange peels, licorice, cardamom, cassia, and grains of paradise.

Of course, where would gin be without tonic? The gin and tonic was born in the English colonies of India and Southeast Asia in the eighteen hundreds. Malaria was a scourge at the time, and quinine, a bitter tonic, was the treatment of choice. The problem was that quinine tasted like doo-doo. To help the medicine go down, a little gin was mixed in. It proved to be quite tasty, and the rest is cocktail history.

Today, any number of other cocktails use gin, from the fruity Singapore Sling to the ever-popular dry martini. And to think, all this sprung from a little old juniper berry.

Q Why does mercury rise or fall depending on the temperature?

A It's a standard cartoon gag: The sun is beating down, eggs are frying on the sidewalk, and people are fanning themselves in overheated agony. Cut to a shot of the thermometer; mercury strains against its glass confines before blowing out the top like water from a geyser. It's exaggerated, but not as much as you may think.

Mercury expands as the temperature increases; as the temperature decreases, it contracts. (If this seems counterintuitive, it's because water reacts to temperature in the opposite way, expanding as it freezes.) As mercury expands, it is channeled upward through the thermometer's thin, hollow center; it will expand as long as the temperature continues to rise, which is why most thermometers have a reservoir at the end.

Daniel Gabriel Fahrenheit—a German glassblower, physicist, and engineer—invented the mercury thermometer in 1714. Fahrenheit chose mercury to gauge changes in temperature for two reasons: The element is liquid at room temperature, and it expands evenly as the temperature rises. Unfortunately, mercury is also quite dangerous—even its vapors are poisonous. That's why, for the most part, digital thermometers have replaced those that are filled with mercury—there always is a chance that glass thermometers will break.

So back to the time-honored cartoon gag, from which you can learn the following lesson: If you notice eggs frying on the sidewalk, be wary of any mercury thermometers you see. Each is like a loaded gun, just waiting for the temperature to get hot enough to make it blow like a toxic Old Faithful.

Q: Why would one person try to get another's goat?

A: The origins of this phrase are surprisingly literal. Indeed, there appears to have been a time in history when, for one reason or another, a person would break into a barn and abscond with another's goat. You can see how this would lead to the present-day usage of the phrase: Waking up in the morning to find yourself one goat poorer than you were the night before would surely be an aggravating experience.

So what's the deal with all of this goat thievery? There are a few possibilities.

Anecdotal evidence suggests that goats were strategically placed in stables that housed racehorses. The presence of a goat was said to have a calming effect on horses, which would thereby perform better at the racetrack. If the goat was removed, the horses became agitated. Racehorses don't perform as well in such a worked-up state, so devious gamblers who were looking for an edge might have tried to get a person's goat in order to affect the outcome of a race.

One source references an older belief that has to do with dairy cows. The goats served the same purpose—providing companionship in the stable. Cows were thought to produce more milk when a goat was hanging around. A rival farmer—or a regular troublemaker—might have tried to get a farmer's goat in order to stunt his cow's production.

A related American idiom, "Don't let them see where your goat is tied," gives some credence to these notions of the phrase's historical origins; if the thieves don't know where to find your goat, they'll have a hard time stealing it. Or, regarding the idiom's common usage, if a person doesn't know what irks you, he'll have a more difficult time making you lose your temper.

A less popular theory cites prison slang as the origin of the expression. Since 1904, at least, "goat" has been substituted for "anger." Thus, to get a person's goat would mean to incite anger. In this context, the phrase gives the same result, but involves fewer animals. The slang may have risen from the belief that goats are angry creatures, prone to lashing out and butting things with their horns.

Wherever the phrase originated—from gamblers, dairy farmers, or inmates—it persists. And attempting to find its exact source has gotten the goat of many a philologist over the years.

Q: Why does organic milk last longer than regular milk?

A: If you obsessively compare expiration dates on dairy products in the grocery store, it may be a sign that you need more hobbies. But if you take a moment to look, you'll probably notice that most regular milk expires within a week or two, while organic milk is usually good for a month or more.

Have organic dairy farmers discovered a breed of cow that is able to produce long-lasting milk? Do the drugs coursing through non-organic dairy cattle shrink their milk's shelf life? The answer to both questions is no—the expiration-date gap comes from differences in the ways that the milk is preserved.

Organic milk producers are dairies that don't use growth hormones, antibiotics, and pesticide-treated food. They stave off spoiling by using ultra-high temperature (UHT) processing. This technique requires the milk to be heated to a scalding 265 to 300 degrees Fahrenheit for a few seconds; this kills all the bacteria. The milk is effectively sterile, and when sealed properly, it can keep for months without being refrigerated (though we don't recommend this). When the carton or bottle is opened, the milk is again exposed to bacteria and is usually good for about two weeks.

Regular milk goes through conventional pasteurization, which isn't as thorough as UHT. In conventional pasteurization, milk is heated to 145 degrees Fahrenheit for half an hour or to 162 degrees Fahrenheit for fifteen seconds. This process doesn't kill everything, but it knocks out enough bacteria to make the milk safe for about two weeks—enough time for the producer to get the milk to the store, the store to sell it, and you to drink it.

Producers of non-organic milk don't use the UHT process because it affects the product's taste. The high temperature burns some sugar in the milk, caramelizing it and giving the milk a sweeter flavor and darker color. To lifelong drinkers of non-organic milk, UHT-processed milk doesn't taste or look quite right.

For most organic dairy companies, conventional pasteurization isn't a viable option. These firms tend to be smaller operations than non-organic dairies, so it may take longer for them to get their milk to retail outlets. What's more, it doesn't sell as quickly as regular milk.

There. Now you don't have to spend a single moment more in the milk aisle than is necessary.

Q: Why do we see our breath on a cold day?

A: Because we are full of hot air. Water exists in three states: as a liquid (water), as a gas (water vapor), and as a solid (ice). Hot air has a greater capacity than cold air to carry moisture—water vapor, that is.

Your breath begins in your lungs, which are warm and wet. When that warm breath leaves your body, it's laden with water vapor. As your breath hits the air on a cold day, the water vapor quickly changes from gas into liquid in the form of tiny water droplets that appear to you as a sort of fog. (Breathe on a cold mirror or window and you get the same effect: Water you can't see coming out of your body suddenly appears on the cold glass surface.)

This is the same process by which moisture on the ground becomes warm, evaporates into water vapor, and rises until it reaches a point in the atmosphere at which the air is cold enough to cause it to re-form into tiny water droplets. Crowd together enough of these water droplets in the sky, and the result is a billowing white mass that is commonly called a cloud.

Q Why doesn't your stomach digest itself?

A Your stomach is the fourth stop on the amazing journey along the digestive tract (after the mouth, pharynx, and esophagus), but it's the point where the system gets down to serious business. Cells in the stomach produce two to three quarts of hydrochloric acid and digestive enzymes daily, and muscles work to churn everything together in order to create a soupy goo. This digestive gastric juice is potent stuff—it's strong enough to break down wood and metal, let alone food. And the only thing that keeps it from eating through your body is a thin layer of equally powerful mucus.

Acids are dangerous because when they are dissolved in water, they release excess hydrogen ions (hydrogen atoms with a positive charge). These ions react easily and quickly with other material, breaking chemical compounds down into simpler compounds. In the stomach, the hydrogen ions combine with protein compounds in food to form amino acids and simpler polypeptide compounds that the small and large intestines can further digest.

The stomach wall is made up of vulnerable proteins, which means that you would be in big trouble if hydrochloric acid were to reach it. Luckily, the stomach surface is lined with cells that continually secrete mucus that neutralizes the acid; this mucus is loaded with bicarbonate, a powerful chemical base. (A base is essentially the opposite of an acid.)

When bicarbonate is dissolved into water, it results in the release of hydroxide ions, which have a negative charge. Negative hydroxide ions and positive hydrogen ions effectively cancel each other out if they are combined; the chemicals undergo a reaction and form water and other harmless products.

The system works well, but since it depends on constant chemical balance, it isn't entirely foolproof. Sometimes acid will erode part of this mucus, resulting in a painful gastric ulcer in the stomach lining. In extreme cases, the acid will erode a hole all the way through the stomach wall, and the stomach's contents will spill out into the abdominal cavity.

Fortunately, the stomach lining keeps most of us safe, even when we eat like pigs. So next Thanksgiving, remember to count mucus among your blessings.

Q Why are school buses yellow?

A If you were hoping to catch a ride to junior high in a bus painted maroon, aqua, or a lovely shade of periwinkle, you're flat out of luck. "School Bus Yellow," as it's commonly known, is a color mandated by United States federal law.

In 1939, Frank W. Cyr, a professor of rural education at Teachers College, Columbia University, organized the country's first national standards conference for school transportation. Before that conference, there weren't any guidelines regarding the construction or color of America's school buses. Through his research, Cyr had discovered that U.S. schoolchildren were being transported to school in vehicles, trucks, and buses of all kinds. In Kansas, one district got kids to school in horse-drawn wheat wagons.

Cyr's conference, which was funded by a five-thousand-dollar grant from the Rockefeller Foundation, took place on April 10–16, 1939, at Teachers College. The attendees were transportation and education officials from the then forty-eight states, as well as engineers and specialists from school bus manufacturing and paint companies, including Chevrolet, Dodge, Ford, DuPont, and Pittsburgh Paint.

Conference participants established numerous construction and mechanical standards for U.S. school buses. Their most memorable (and long-standing) accomplishment was the selection of yellow as the standard national color for the transports. With safety as the first objective, the particular shade of yellow was chosen because it is easiest for motorists to see in the dim conditions of early morning, late afternoon, and bad weather.

The color became officially known as "National School Bus Chrome," and it remains a school bus safety attribute that is mandated by federal law. Scientific studies show that yellow commands people's attention faster than any other color—even when it's out of our peripheral vision. For the record, Cyr, Father of the Yellow School Bus, thought that the color more resembled a shade of orange.

Why Are There More Women Than Men? • 233

Q: Why do most sports go counterclockwise?

A: For most nonathletes living their quiet day-to-day lives, doing things clockwise seems pretty intuitive. Doorknobs turn clockwise, screws are tightened clockwise, and yes, clocks run clockwise. Board games usually move clockwise, blackjack dealers hand out cards clockwise, and people in restaurants usually take turns ordering in a clockwise direction.

Yet in many of our sports, such as baseball and all types of racing, play moves in a counterclockwise direction. This can cause some serious confusion for clockwise-oriented individuals—just ask any T-ball coach trying to shepherd a young hitter down the first-base line.

How did this counterintuitive situation come to be? Part of the answer is rooted in history, of course. In ancient times, when the Roman Empire ruled virtually the entire known Western world, a popular form of entertainment was chariot racing. As Charlton Heston fans know, chariot racing moved in a counterclockwise direction.

Roman horses were invaluable in war and were trained to turn to the left to give right-handed spear-wielding riders an advantage in battle; in the Circus Maximus, it was natural to build the track to suit this. Considering the power of habit in human social development, it seems reasonable to assume that future forms of racing simply adopted the same direction of travel as the mighty Romans.

Some science-minded individuals postulate that foot racing goes counterclockwise due to physical forces. Because most people are right-handed (and right-footed), a counterclockwise motion tends to help those with a dominant right leg speed around turns. This is because of centrifugal force, which we're sure everybody remembers from high school physics. For those who have forgotten (or never knew), centrifugal force is that sense of momentum—called inertia—that tries to keep you going in a straight line when you're trying to turn. A right-legged individual moving counterclockwise, this explanation contends, will have a better chance of counteracting this force.

Some sports move the other way. In England, for example, horse races travel in a clockwise direction. This seems particularly baffling, considering that American horse racing—which was brought over by the British during colonial times—moves counterclockwise. It turns out, though, that counterclockwise horse racing actually developed in the United States in response to the British tradition.

One of the first American horse tracks built after the Revolutionary War was established in 1780 by Kentuckian William Whitley. Flushed with pride at the newly won independence of the colonies, Whitley declared that horse racing in the new country should go in the opposite direction of those stodgy, tyrannical Brits.

Baseball, in which runners move counterclockwise around the bases, also may have descended from a British ancestor. Some baseball historians have postulated that the modern national pastime may be based on a British bat-and-ball game called rounders. Interestingly, rounders players moved in a clockwise direction around the bases; why this was reversed in the rules of baseball is not known.

Possibly, the counterclockwise movement has to do with the orientation of the diamond. It's far easier for righthanders to throw across the diamond to first base if the runner is moving in a counterclockwise direction (which is also why you almost never see lefthanders playing any infield positions except for first base).

Of course, from one perspective, clockwise and counterclockwise are meaningless terms. Some physicists enjoy pointing out (somewhat smugly, we might add) that direction is entirely relative. Which means that those seemingly confused T-ball toddlers might be a lot smarter than we think.

Q: Why do we say "head over heels in love"?

A: You can coo this phrase to your lover when the mood strikes, but let's hope that neither of you thinks about it literally. After all, the sentiment is pretty mundane, even flatly obvious—we spend almost every waking moment with our heads over our heels. So what's so special about you, Romeo?

You might as well say, "I'm so crazy about you that I often find myself seated comfortably upright" or "You're on my mind so much lately that I routinely get eight hours of sleep, three square meals a day, and a reasonable amount of exercise." Regardless of what common sense tells you the phrase should describe, "head over heels" is commonly understood to mean something quite the opposite. Much like "topsy-turvy" or "upside down," it's supposed to convey an air of craziness or an unsettled equilibrium.

The original version of the phrase, dating to the fourteenth century, is much more accurate: "heels over head." It was used to describe the precarious moment that you experience while turning a somersault or a cartwheel, when your heels are quite literally suspended over your head.

How this got corrupted is anybody's guess, but by the late seventeen hundreds, the more prosaic "head over heels" began to appear in literature. The earliest identified use of the phrase to describe being in love came in 1834, in Davy Crockett's *Narrative of the Life of Davy Crockett*.

Does it make much sense? No. But neither does love—it's the most confusing and illogical of human emotions. So in that respect, the words are perfect just the way they are.

Q: Why do we cross our fingers for good luck?

A: Humans are a superstitious bunch. We won't walk under ladders. We avoid black cats. We greet Friday the thirteenth with extreme fear and trepidation. And when we need an extra jolt of good luck—when, say, we're confronted with a ladder, a black cat, or Friday the thirteenth—we cross our fingers. Why is this?

Tradition connects the gesture to the Christian sign of the cross. In earlier times, people saw supernatural evil just about everywhere they looked. They often attributed illness and misfortune to the influences of evil forces, and they expected to find spirits, witches, and other supernatural pests lurking around every corner. When they stumbled upon evil, it was common practice to call on divine protection by making the sign of the cross (touching the forehead, then the chest, then the left and right shoulders in turn).

It's possible that crossed fingers were originally meant as a similar appeal for God's protection. By subtly forming a cross with the index and middle fingers, a frightened Christian wouldn't attract undue attention. After all, you wouldn't want the neighborhood witch to know you were on to her—she might turn you into a mule or dispatch gophers to ravage your garden.

Finger crossing may predate the symbolism of the Christian cross. Some New Age spiritualists trace the gesture to a pagan practice in which two people would form a cross with each other's index fingers and then make a wish. In this case, the crossed fingers would have probably evoked the solar cross, an astrological sign that features an equilateral cross inside a ring and dates back to prehistoric times.

The solar cross was, among other things, associated with nature, earth, the sun, and divinity. According to this line of thinking, pagans believed that good spirits existed at the center of a perfect cross and that they could trap a wish there by making a cross with their fingers.

The practice of finger crossing continues to this day, even if we talk about it more than we actually do it. In fact, the phrase "keep your fingers crossed" dates back only to the 1920s. Even with the major strides we've made in understanding the universe around us, we remain, apparently, every bit as superstitious as our ancient ancestors were.

Q Why do we sweat?

A Human sweat glands are like a built-in sprinkler system. Sweat enables us to cool off when the exterior temperature rises (due to changes in the weather) or when our interior temperatures rise (due to exercise, anxiety, or illness). Sweat is one of the mechanisms that our bodies use to keep us at a steady—and healthy—98.6 degrees Fahrenheit.

Here are the basics: Humans have about 2.6 million sweat glands, but not all of these glands produce the same kind of sweat. Sweat has two distinct sources: eccrine and apocrine glands. Eccrine glands exist all over the body and are active from birth. They constantly release a salty, nearly odorless fluid onto the skin, though you probably only notice this sweat when it's really hot or you've been working out really hard.

Apocrine glands, on the other hand, are concentrated in the armpits, on the soles of the feet, in the palms of the hands, and in the groin. They become active during puberty. Yes, puberty and perspiration go hand in hand.

Apocrine glands don't secrete liquid directly onto the skin. Instead, each gland empties into a hair follicle. When a person is under emotional or physical stress, the tiny muscle around the hair follicle contracts, pushing the liquid onto the skin, where it becomes sweat. Apocrine glands carry lipids and proteins, as well as water and salt. When these substances mix with the sebaceous oils in the hair follicles and then meet the bacteria on the skin, well, that's when you begin to hold your nose.

But before you start thinking of eccrine as "good" sweat and apocrine as "bad," consider this little nugget of information: Apocrine sweat has been found to contain androsterone pheromones, those mysterious musky odors that are responsible for sexual arousal. So sweat can be sexy, too. Just don't take this as an excuse to wear unwashed gym socks on a date—a few pheromones go a long way.

To banish body odor, a little dab of deodorant should do. Deodorants are based on mildly acidic compounds that dry the skin before the odor starts. Antiperspirants, another popular option, actually block sweat with aluminum salts. Some people think that these salts may be unhealthy, but so far, clinical evidence has failed to connect them to any disease.

If you feel that you sweat too much, or too little, see your doctor. Excessive sweating, officially known as hyperhidrosis, and lack of sweat, called anhidrosis, are genuine medical conditions with serious complications. Fortunately, both are treatable.

For most of us, however, dealing with sweat is fairly simple: Take a shower and wear loose and absorbent clothing. For goodness sake, don't sweat about sweat!

Q Why do people dress up their pets?

A People dress up their pets for several reasons—some of which are practical, others psychological.

On the practical side, certain breeds of dogs don't have enough meat on their bones or fur in their coats to keep themselves warm in cold weather, so you can buy little coats or wraps to help them stay warm. Of course, you can also buy your dog a bathing suit, though there's no physiological need for it.

Indeed, Web sites sell thousands of doggie Halloween costumes, from pirates to princesses, Superman to Darth Vader. Yes, we humans find animals cute, and some of us find them even cuter when they are dressed to the nines.

And this brings us to the psychological part of the equation. Many people consider a pet to be a member of the family; some nutty folks even treat their pets as equals. Perhaps that helps explain why Americans in 2008 spent in the neighborhood of forty-three billion dollars on their dogs, cats, horses, hamsters, rabbits, and occasionally squirrels. Yes, you read that astounding number correctly.

So, why else might we be putting capes on our dogs or Santa Claus hats on our cats? One study suggests that it may be because we are lonely. In research conducted at the University of Chicago, ninety-nine people were asked to describe their own pet or the pet of someone they knew. The lonelier the people were in their everyday lives, the more likely they were to use human traits to describe their pets, employing such words as "thoughtful" and "sympathetic."

The lesson is clear: We are social creatures, and when the need to connect with other humans is not fulfilled, we seek out ways to fill the void. For some of use, Mr. Fluffy clad in a woolly sweater fits the bill.

Q: Why do airplane seats need to be "fully upright" for takeoff and landing?

A: You're taking the red-eye home from vacation so you can get to work on time the next morning. Minutes into the flight, you have a pillow tucked under your head and your seat reclined in just the right position—you're dozing before the twinkling lights on the ground have even faded to black. Before you know it, the flight attendant is telling you that the plane will be landing shortly and that you need to return your seat to the standard upright position. You don't remember asking for the complimentary wake-up call, so why are you being pestered?

As with many of life's minor irritations, the underlying concept is safety. The Federal Aviation Administration (FAA) requires that all seats be in the standard upright and locked position immediately prior to the takeoff and landing of a commercial airliner. (Which is why, when you ask for five more minutes, the flight attendant doesn't let you roll over and go back to sleep.) Most emergency situations occur as a plane is preparing for takeoff or coming in for a landing, and if disaster strikes, the FAA wants each passenger to have as clear a route to the emergency exits as possible.

In economy class, the average seat "pitch" (the distance between a point on your seat and the same point on the seat directly behind or in front of you) is between thirty-one and thirty-four inches. That's not much real estate. A reclined seat drastically reduces the freedom of movement of the passenger behind you. Add an open tray table to the mix, and the escape route begins to resemble an obstacle course. (Seats in the row in front of the emergency exits don't recline, allowing for better access in case of emergency.)

So the next time you've muffled the flight attendant's voice by holding your pillow over your ears, mistaken her nose for the snooze button on your alarm clock, and told yourself that it's only a dream and that you're still in your five-star hotel room, try to shake yourself awake and follow the poor woman's instructions. After that, apologize for batting her nose. Then avoid making eye contact with her for the rest of the flight.

Q Why is red wine served at room temperature and white wine chilled?

A Would you enjoy lukewarm lemonade or not-so-hot hot chocolate? Didn't think so.

Researchers at Belgium's Katholieke Universiteit Leuven have discovered that our taste buds perceive flavors differently at different temperatures. Specifically, the warmer the food or beverage in your mouth is, the stronger the electric flavor signal that travel from your taste receptors to your brain are. This can be a good or a bad thing, depending on what you're eating or drinking. For example, frozen ice cream tastes sweeter as it melts on your tongue, but a beer tastes bitter after it's gotten warm in the sun.

But back to the grape juice. The whole point of chilling (or not chilling) a wine is to serve it at a temperature at which our taste buds will be most tantalized by it. Cold makes white wines less sweet and more refreshingly crisp and acidic, and helps champagnes and sparklers retain their bubbles long after you've popped the cork. Reds tend to be a bit more tannic (biting) than whites, so a little warmth goes a long way in making them taste more fruity and aromatic.

Wine snobs (okay, "wine experts") will tell you that the proper serving temperature is crucial to bringing out a wine's optimal flavor, aroma, and structure (how it feels on your tongue). Frankly, some of these people can get a little obsessed. They will spout out general rules such as these: Sparkling wine must be served at forty-eight degrees Fahrenheit, white wine at fifty-three degrees Fahrenheit, rosé wine at fifty-one degrees Fahrenheit, and red wine at sixty-two degrees Fahrenheit.

The experts have the best intentions. After all, serving a wine too warm or too cold can negatively affect its flavor. A white that's overly frigid can taste... well, tasteless. And a red that's too toasty can seem too alcoholic, even vinegary.

What's a wine drinker without a fancy wine cellar to do? First of all, don't lose any sleep over the precise optimal serving temperature for your favorite Two-Buck Chuck. Just follow this super-simple rule of thumb from wine educator Mark Oldman (*Oldman's Guide to Outsmarting Wine*): Fifteen minutes before serving time, take white wines out of the fridge and pop the red ones in.

Q: Why do we carve jack-o'-lanterns?

A: Who doesn't fondly remember the Halloweens of yore? You'd choose a big orange pumpkin from a local farm, cut off the top to scoop out the mushy insides, and spend an entire evening painstakingly carving out the features. Then finally, with tired eyes, aching fingers, and a sense of pride, you'd place your glowing work of art on the front porch... where it would last about 18.4 minutes before some kid would smash it into smithereens.

Though the practice seems somewhat futile in our pumpkin-smashing present, the tradition of carving jack-o'-lanterns dates back centuries. There is no definitive explanation for how present-day jack-o'-lanterns came into being, but we do know that ancient Celts—as well as other sects of the era—believed that flames would ward off evil spirits.

In the Celtic tradition, the harvest season ended on November 1. This date, according to Celtic legend, also signified a dangerous event: a time when the boundary between the living and dead blurred. For one day, potentially harmful spirits could wreak havoc on the living. To keep these spirits at bay, ancient people built large bonfires as part of their end-of-harvest festivals—festivals that live on today as Halloween celebrations.

But why do we carve jack-o'-lanterns? In the absence of documented evidence, most people cite an Irish folktale called "Stingy Jack." In a small Irish village, the legend goes, lived a deceitful, lying, drunken fellow named Jack. He was also a cheap bastard, so he was known to the locals as Stingy Jack. One evening, Stingy Jack, out on a drunken spree, ran into the devil, who informed Jack that due to his derelict behavior, he was going to hell. The devil asked Jack to kindly prepare his soul to be taken. Jack suggested a drink beforehand. The devil—apparently a truly Irish evil spirit—agreed.

When the bill came, the devil and Stingy Jack looked at each other awkwardly. Stingy Jack reminded the devil of his nickname and said that he had a reputation to uphold. The devil informed Jack that Lucifer, Lord of Hell, didn't buy people drinks. The barkeeper said he didn't care who they were—no one drank for free.

They were at a stalemate, but then Jack had an idea: What if the devil transformed himself into a silver coin with which Jack would pay their bill? The devil, who had perhaps had a few too many drinks, inexplicably thought this to be a brilliant idea. Upon transformation, though, Jack promptly put the numismatic devil into his pocket, along with a silver crucifix to prevent the devil from reverting to form. It was only after he extracted a promise from the devil to not take his soul that Jack released the captive demon.

Much later, when Stingy Jack died, he was denied entrance to heaven. The devil also refused him entrance at the gates of hell, citing the promise he had made long before. He did, however, offer Jack a perpetually glowing piece of coal. Stingy Jack was doomed to wander the countryside for eternity, with nothing but his glowing coal from hell to light the way.

To ward off the spirit of Stingy Jack—also known as "Jack of the Lantern"—people in ancient Ireland, Scotland, and England began to carve scary faces into hollowed-out turnips and potatoes. When the first British settlers came to North America, legend suggests that they continued the tradition, using the native North American pumpkin. It was, after all, larger, simpler to carve, and easier to smash into smithereens.

Q Why do we have to "face the music"?

A At some point, we all have to accept the consequences of our actions and "face the music." Thankfully, there's rarely an actual soundtrack involved when we take our punishments. Being forced to listen to Britney Spears while our bosses chew us out would be unnecessarily cruel. But according to lore, there was indeed real music involved when people first used the expression.

There are two common stories that are associated with the origin of this phrase. The first suggests that the saying grew out of the theater. When actors went out to ham it up under the red-hot spotlights, they were facing the pit orchestra at the front of the stage—they were literally facing the music. But given the way that we use the phrase today, this explanation doesn't make much sense. Sure, facing a potentially hostile audience is nerve-wracking, but it doesn't have anything to do with accepting the consequences of one's actions. And don't actors want to go out on stage?

The second explanation is probably a better fit. The story goes that when a soldier was dismissed from an army in disgrace, he would have to take part in a "drumming out" ceremony. As he was stripped of his rank and excised from his brotherhood, the military band would play the "Rogue's March"—the quintessential drum tune of shame. (In one version of this story, the disgraced soldier would actually have to ride away sitting backward on his horse, presumably to better take in the scorn of his former compatriots.) So facing this music was synonymous with facing public shame and humiliation.

But this explanation isn't definitive, either. Maybe we should quit wondering about the phrase's origin and just be happy that our own public disgraces don't involve military drummers or pit orchestras. Shame is bad enough without a theme song.

Q Why does the U.S. president pardon a turkey each Thanksgiving?

A George H. W. Bush knows the answer, because he started the tradition. In 1989, he granted a presidential pardon to a turkey. Perhaps he was feeling benevolent, or maybe he wished to make the two hundredth presidential Thanksgiving proclamation memorable. Maybe Bush just liked the bird... or disliked roast turkey. It might have been to please the many children who had come to watch the National Turkey Federation (NTF) deliver the bird to the White House. Whatever the reason, every president since has pardoned a turkey before Thanksgiving Day.

Many turkey observers claim that the tradition began earlier. In 1963, John F. Kennedy announced that he would not eat the turkey he received. "We'll just let this one grow," he lightheartedly told reporters before returning the fifty-five-pound bird to the farm. Newspapers reported it as a "pardon," but subsequent presidents didn't follow Kennedy's lead.

Some sources, including the White House Web site, credit Harry Truman with starting the pardon tradition in 1947. But the Truman Library disagrees, saying that 1947 was merely the first year that the NTF began to provide birds to the White House. The buck may have stopped at Truman's desk, but not the axe.

Abraham Lincoln might have been the first president to pardon a turkey, but it didn't trigger a tradition. In the middle of the Civil War, Lincoln proclaimed the first official Thanksgiving holiday. Thanksgiving had been observed since the days of the Pilgrims, but different parts of the country celebrated it on different days. Lincoln took advice from Sarah Josepha Hale, editor of a popular magazine, *Godey's Lady's Book*: She had urged him to select a specific day for the holiday. In October 1863, Lincoln signed a proclamation that designated the last Thursday in November as a national day of thanksgiving and praise.

Lincoln's proclamation is a fact, but there's more to the turkey part of the story. It seems Lincoln's youngest son, Tad, adopted a turkey named Jack (Tom, in some tellings) and trained the bird to eat from his hand and follow him around. When the holiday approached and Tad learned that the turkey was fated to a dinner platter, he panicked. The boy burst into a cabinet meeting to plead for Jack's life. Lincoln responded with a reprieve.

In any event, turkeydom had to wait 126 years for another Republican, George Herbert Walker Bush, to free a gobbling White House guest from the axe and begin a tradition that's stuck. We here at Q&A headquarters are a sentimental bunch—we like to think that he did it for the kiddies.

 Why should I mind my P's and Q's?

 Didn't you grow up with a proper English nanny? In the United Kingdom, minding your P's and Q's refers to watching your manners. And we all know what happens when you don't behave your best. You get a slap on the bum—or at least a lengthy stay on the naughty stool.

Some experts contend that the phrase "mind your P's and Q's" evolved as an abbreviation for "mind your pleases and thank-yous." However, on the U.S. side of the pond, minding your P's and Q's has a second meaning: It's a reminder to be alert and in stellar form.

Not minding your P's and Q's can result in several calamities, including egregious spelling errors, a swift scolding from your dance instructor, or a surcharge at the pub. You see, no one can really agree on which exact P's and Q's we should be minding. From an etymological standpoint, many different explanations have been passed down through the years.

One theory claims that "mind your P's and Q's" was intended to get kids "to learn one's [handwritten] letters." For schoolchildren beginning to write, it might have served as a sort of mnemonic aid, a short way to say: "Be careful not to mix up your lowercase p's and q's, little ones! Those crafty characters are exact mirror images of each other. And you don't want to spell *puid qro puo* when you really mean *quid pro quo*."

But is this nifty piece of penmanship advice the true origin of "mind your P's and Q's"? Detractors—mostly people who point out that similar spelling problems could occur by not minding your b's and d's—say no. So just what are the P's and Q's in question? Could they be the dance figures *pieds* and *queues*? Austere French dance masters might say *oui*, but the *Oxford English Dictionary* says no.

What about pints and quarts? Ah, now you're onto something. According to the *Origin of Navy Terminology*, the phrase "mind your P's and Q's" has nautical beginnings. It says, "In the days of sail when sailors were paid a pittance," seamen drank beer in taverns that were willing to extend them credit until payday. The barmen kept chalkboards behind the bar and marked a "P" for pint and a "Q" for quart next to each person's name for each draught ordered.

This was a great reason to keep careful track of your P's and Q's. Paying attention to how many pints and quarts you drank ensured an accurate payday tab from a less-than-scrupulous barman and kept you out of financial trouble. Of course, staying semi-sober also makes it a bit easier to keep your behavior under control. And though no one knows the exact meaning or origin of this quirky catchphrase, one thing's for sure: If you mind your P's and Q's—all of them—you'll stay out of trouble. And your nanny would certainly be pleased with that.

Q: Why do we tip some service people but not others?

A: The practical reason is that tipping is built into the pay structure for certain jobs. In the United States, employers set wages for certain jobs with the expectation that tips will be a big part of an employee's income. These jobs include restaurant food servers, food-delivery drivers, bartenders, hair stylists, hotel housekeepers, bellhops, taxi drivers, and valets. In many cases, base pay for these jobs is less than minimum wage, and gratuities make up the difference.

You may see tip jars at, say, coffee shops, but Americans don't feel societal pressure to tip on every visit to these establishments. Nor do the livelihoods of the baristas depend on tips. In full-service restaurants, on the other hand, most people know that you should tip a server 15 to 20 percent and that the server depends on this money.

Where did these rules come from? For many "tipping professions," the tradition dates back to the English aristocracy in the seventeenth and eighteenth centuries. When the well-to-do visited each other's estates for extended periods, they typically rewarded the host's servants with "vails"—something extra at the end of stays as thanks for tending to the rooms and other needs. (It would have been simply dreadful not to pay the help. What would it have said about one's own assets?) This type of peer pressure eventually forced vails into common practice at commercial establishments.

The practice took hold among the well-to-do in the United States following the Civil War. Though many people publicly condemned the practice as anti-American because it seemed to propagate the notion of rigidly separated classes, tipping gradually spread beyond homes to the equivalents of domestic servers, maids, valets, and others at inns and restaurants. Americans also began to tip for some additional services (i.e., shoe shining, coat checks, taxis).

Today, tipping traditions are associated with the type of service and not with the wealth of the customer. Eating at the Waffle House may be a far cry from fine dining among the English aristocracy, but Waffle House servers are still part of a tradition that began on seventeenth-century estates. Fast-food workers, on the other hand, don't tend to your needs during a meal, so they fall in the tradition of street vendors, in which tipping never took root. Of course, if you buck the trend and tip them anyway, you might get an extra ketchup packet out of the deal.

Q Why does reading in the car make you sick?

A The theory goes that motion sickness is a physical response to a perceived paradox; in other words, it's your body saying, "This does not compute." Conflicting information is transmitted by separate receptors: One says that you're moving, while the other says that you're not. Your stomach winds up being the loser of the debate, and the results can include nausea and vomiting.

Your body has various methods of determining its position and state of motion. One is a set of receptors in the inner ear that controls your balance. When fluid inside the cochlea moves, it stimulates the tiny hairs that grow there. The movement of these hairs notifies your brain when you are listing to the left, tilting to the right, or leaning into a powerful wind. These hairs also detect when your body is in motion. The eyes comprise another set of receptors that is important to establishing motion. When you see trees flying by on either side, you can be pretty sure that it is your body that is moving and not the forest.

When you read in the car (or play a handheld video game or look at a map for an extended time), your gaze is focused on a fixed point. According to the stimuli that are recorded by your visual receptors, your body is at rest. "But, no!" protests your inner ear.

"Of course we're still moving!" The tiny hairs, which sway as you bump and jostle, send the message of movement to the brain.

Faced with this paradox, the brain overloads. Dizziness ensues; the stomach is upset; and, if it's a severe case, lunch is lost. And it's all because of an argument between two stubborn sensory receptors, neither of which will admit to being wrong.

Fortunately, motion sickness is common enough to warrant readily available medication that can prevent the nausea from taking hold in the first place. But what if you don't take any medication before settling into the backseat of a car and reading this compelling book? If you start to feel queasy, raise your eyes from these pages and look at the horizon. Showing your eyes that, yes, you are indeed moving will settle both the argument and, eventually, your stomach.

That is, until you start reading again. The eyes are forgetful little beasts—they'll soon return to thinking that you are standing still, and the debate will rage all over again.

Q: Why do we trick-or-treat?

A: When you stop to think about it, trick-or-treating is a bit strange. We dress as a vampire, a princess, or a member of the opposite sex, then traipse from house to house, ringing doorbells and demanding treats. Most of the year, you'd get arrested for that kind of behavior. (Trust us.) But on Halloween, you're rewarded with candy.

Most historians agree that Halloween is derived from the ancient Celtic festival Samhain, which is held annually on November 1 to mark the end of the harvest season. The Celts believed that on the night before the festival, spirits of the dead were set free in the world of the living. To protect themselves, the Celts performed various rituals, such as building large bonfires. They also wore scary costumes—a precursor, some folklorists suggest, to our modern-day tradition of dressing up for Halloween.

Though humans have played dress-up for thousands of years, it was the British and Irish who struck upon the particular genius of donning a costume and then demanding gifts. From medieval times to well into the twentieth century, British islanders participated in the holiday tradition of "mumming"—prancing through the neighborhood in costume and asking for food and drink in exchange for a performance of a short play or song.

In Northern Ireland, in particular, this tradition continues with "Halloween rhyming," in which costumed children go door-to-door singing songs and hoping for a few pennies in return. During the massive Irish immigration to the United States in the late nineteenth and early twentieth centuries, immigrants brought along their Halloween traditions, including costumes.

Folklorists and historians are uncertain how a pleasant exchange of entertainment for pennies turned into the thinly disguised extortion of the American version. It appears the American custom of trick-or-treating didn't fully take hold until well into the twentieth century. The *Oxford English Dictionary* found the first use of the phrase "trick or treat" in print in 1947. That's not to say trick-or-treating was instantly accepted. In October 1954, a grumpy *Baltimore Sun* newspaper writer implored, "Now that the 'Trick-or-

Treat' season is upon us, let us hope that thoughtful parents will discourage the practice."

It goes without saying that thoughtful parents did nothing of the sort. We have the Tootsie Rolls to prove it.

Q: Why is salt both good and bad for you?

A: As with everything—alcohol, sun, Adam Sandler movies—the key is moderation. Salt can certainly be bad for you, but you also need it to stay alive. Salt is derived from sodium chloride, which is essential for keeping your body chemistry balanced. Basically, sodium chloride regulates where water is distributed and absorbed in the body.

Every day, Americans eat twice as much salt as nutritionists recommend, according to the American Medical Association. So the good news is that most people are in no danger of getting too little sodium chloride. This is somewhat fortunate, since sodium deficiency can cause too much water to enter the bloodstream and travel to the brain, which could lead to convulsions, dizziness, muscle cramps, confusion, and possibly a coma or death. In short, if you don't have enough salt, you will overdose on water.

The bad news is that too much salt can create nasty problems, too, particularly for people who are born with a high salt sensitivity—a predisposition to high blood pressure. For these folks, salt is a serious health issue. (If you have high blood pressure, cutting back on salt can significantly reduce your chances of having a heart attack or stroke.) Too much salt can also lead to heartburn, ulcers, kidney stones, and other health problems.

So while sodium chloride is definitely important for your survival, it's not a great idea to tie a salt lick around your neck for constant access. Leave that to goats and other farm animals.

Q: Why do parties always end up in the kitchen?

A: Because that's where the food comes from, friendly reader. Why wait for the tray of canapés to make its way from the kitchen through the dining room, past the great room and out onto the deck? By the time it gets to you, here's what will be left: some crumbs of Chex mix, one lousy pig in a blanket, and a teeny-tiny cucumber sandwich that doesn't really count as a sandwich anyway because it doesn't have a top or deli meat.

No, the smartest partygoers stake out a spot in the kitchen right by the range. Not so close that they feel the heat, mind you, but close enough to get first dibs on the cranberry-baked Brie at its oozing best right out of the oven.

Besides, hanging in the kitchen gives you a chance to chat with the hostess instead of with Larry the drill-bit salesman. In the olden days, the hostess might have been slaving away for the entirety of the party. But not anymore. Today, she's a liberated at-home chef who is surrounded by four hundred square feet of hardwood floors, designer cabinet knobs, and sparkling stainless steel appliances (Sub-Zero, of course). Her kitchen is no longer a solitary workspace—it's the showpiece of her home. And she certainly doesn't mind showing it off to all her guests.

Go ahead, indulge her. Why not offer to slice a tomato or garnish the cheese ball? You can even dip your chips in the chipotle salsa without fear of dripping on the living room carpet, and sip Chardonnay from a real wine glass rather than one of those plastic two-parters with the detachable stem. You probably can even keep up with the Notre Dame game on the countertop flat-screen TV.

Best of all, being in the kitchen means that once the party hits full force, your stomach will be so full of food that the alcohol you're drinking won't get the best of you. So drink up. There's no way you'll dance with a lampshade on your head. Leave that to Larry.

Q: Why do ostriches stick their heads in the sand?

A: The truth is that they don't. But this myth is pretty much par for the course for the much-maligned ostrich.

Ostriches have one of the worst reputations in the animal kingdom: They are reputed to be stupid, cowardly, and neglectful as parents. The bird gets the neglectful rap because it runs when threatened, even if doing so means leaving its eggs vulnerable. (Often, though, the predator chases the adult ostrich, and the eggs remain unharmed.) In the Book of Job in the Old Testament, the ostrich is used to demonstrate how a man should not live his life; the tome even goes as far as to say that the ostrich is the only animal that does not love its progeny.

And what about the head-in-the-sand bit? It probably has its roots in Pliny the Elder's *Natural History*, from the first century AD. Pliny, an ancient Roman naturalist and philosopher, reported that the ostrich would hide its head in a bush at the first sign of danger, and that by doing so, the animal believed that its entire body was out of sight.

The truth is less prosaic, but no more respectable: At the first sign of danger, an ostrich will flee or, if it is unable to run, flop on the ground and stretch its neck out in the dirt. Here we have another possible origin for the myth—an ostrich's head and neck are roughly the same hue as sand, so when it is flat on the ground, the head and neck are somewhat camouflaged. A person, then, might not see the head at all, which could lead to the belief that the ostrich buried it in the ground.

Another theory is based on the fact that ostriches—like most birds—swallow small stones to aid in the digestive process. To reach these stones, an ostrich must lower its long neck to the ground. Again, this can look as if the ostrich is attempting to bury its head.

Although there isn'tt an ounce of truth to the "head in the sand" adage, you can count on hearing it in everything from political speeches to religious sermons. It's a potent metaphor for a person who would rather hide from his problems than face them. As for the ostrich itself? Well, it continues to have image problems aplenty. In fact, after being called a fool, a coward, and a rotten parent, it's surprising that the bird doesn't bury its head in the sand in shame.

Q Why does K stand for strikeout?

A To the uninitiated, a baseball scorecard can look like hieroglyphs in need of the Rosetta stone: numbers, circles, lines, colored diamonds, and more abbreviations than an IM conversation between hyperactive teens. And when the seven-dollar beers start flowing in the grandstand—forget about it.

Actually, most of these abbreviations are fairly easy to decipher. It doesn't take a sabermetrician to figure out that HR stands for "home run" and BB stands for "base on balls." But what genius designated K the symbol for "strikeout"?

That would be Henry Chadwick—writer, National Baseball Hall of Fame member, and inventor of the baseball box score. Chadwick was born in England in 1824 and grew up as an avid fan of the English ball games cricket and rounders. He emigrated to the United States as a young man, and in the 1850s, as the relatively new sport of baseball gained popularity in America, Chadwick became a devoted fan. Chadwick was a newspaper reporter in New York at the time, and at his urging, the city's major newspapers added coverage of baseball games to their agendas.

A lot happens in a baseball game, and Chadwick knew that it wasn't always easy to keep track of what was going on—especially when the thirteen-cent beers started flowing in the grandstand. In 1861, in a treatise curiously titled *Beadle's Dime Base-Ball Player*, Chadwick introduced a scorecard for baseball games. It was adapted from one used by reporters to keep track of cricket matches.

Chadwick's early scorecard was an unwieldy, Excel-worthy spreadsheet. It involved twenty-nine columns that were thirteen rows deep, and provided space for stats of the day like "bounds" and "muffs." It also included space to record what happened on a play-to-play basis, which helped writers recreate the game in the next day's newspaper.

Because S was so common in baseball's statistical lexicon ("stolen base," "sacrifice," "strikeout"), Chadwick chose K to represent the whiff. Why K? It's the last letter in "struck," which was the common term that was used to describe the strikeout in the 1860s.

The baseball scorecard has grown more comprehensible over the years, but much of Chadwick's original form and symbolism survives, including the use of K for a strikeout. Nowadays, many fans take it further by using a normal K to represent a swinging strikeout and a backward K to represent a called third strike.

Chadwick, who devoted his life to promoting baseball, would no doubt delight at the immense popularity the game has attained. It's doubtful that he'd be impressed by the beer sales, however: Chadwick was a strong supporter of the temperance movement.

Q Why don't we run out of water?

A Because Earth is one big water storage and recycling system. The amount of water on the planet is more or less constant—it's just continually changing form. The process is known as the water cycle.

The water cycle includes a variety of different paths, but it basically goes like this: When the sun heats the oceans, lakes, and rivers, water evaporates from their surfaces and forms water vapor. The process of evaporation eliminates the salt and impurities from seawater, leaving clean freshwater in gaseous form.

Some water vapor rises high in the atmosphere, cools, and condenses into tiny liquid droplets and ice that form clouds. Sometimes the liquid droplets and ice in the clouds grow big enough to fall as rain, sleet, snow, and hail. The portion of this precipitation that collects on land soaks into the ground and flows into lakes, streams, and rivers, eventually making its way back to the oceans.

We use this water to sustain life, of course, and to keep our Slip 'n' Slides slick and our cars shiny. But when we use water, we're usually just passing it through something (like our bodies) or adding stuff to it. We're not changing the actual water molecules, which remain part of the water cycle.

It's a pretty good system, but there's a catch: Yes, there is a massive, constant volume of water on the planet, but the vast majority is tied up in storage at any one time. Most of it exists in some form that is of little use to us—about 97 percent of Earth's water is undrinkable saltwater and about 2.1 percent is frozen in glaciers and icecaps. That leaves only about 0.9 percent in freshwater form, and much of that is underground, inaccessible to us. So while nature takes care of continually replenishing the freshwater supply, it leaves us a limited amount to use at any one time.

This is a problem because we're dangerously close to exceeding the rate at which nature can recycle water, even with help from modern water treatment facilities. In a sense, nature is up against a manmade consumption cycle: Modern agriculture and industry pollute a lot of water, which reduces the freshwater supply, while at the same time the demand for water is increasing as Earth's population continues to grow—and this growth compels agriculture and industry to expand.

Water shortages are at crisis levels in parts of Africa and Asia. Many scientists believe that the United States and much of the rest of the world will be in a similar predicament within fifty years unless we make some major changes. In this frightening scenario, the planet won't run out of water in the long-term—but it might in the short-term. If this comes to pass, a dry Slip 'n Slide will be the least of our problems.

Q Why is the bald eagle the U.S. national bird?

A After the U.S. founding fathers kicked the Brits out and hung up the "Under New Management" sign, they needed a few essential accessories: a system of government to run the joint, a flag to identify its ships, and a Great Seal for authenticating international treaties and agreements.

Oddly enough, the Great Seal turned out to be a tricky one: Jefferson, Franklin, Adams, and the gang started spitballing ideas on July 4, 1776. During the next six years, three different committees pitched designs, but Congress rejected all of them. In 1782, Congress gave the three unsatisfactory proposals to the Secretary of the Continental Congress, Charles Thomson, and asked him to take a crack at it.

Thomson liked certain elements from each of the earlier attempts, including a small white eagle from the third committee. As a history and classics buff, he knew that eagles had a long history as national emblems. Roman soldiers carried eagle-topped staffs into battle; medieval knights slapped them on their family coats of arms; and Germany, Russia, and Poland adopted them as national symbols.

But while he liked the iconic nobility and strength of the eagle, Thomson thought it was important that the U.S. symbol be something unique to America, to underscore the young nation's independence from Europe. So he changed the bird to the bald eagle, which is indigenous to North America. (Incidentally, "bald" doesn't have anything to do with hair loss in this case—the term dates back to the thirteenth century and describes white coloration on the head.)

After less than a week of brainstorming, Thomson gave his ideas to one of the more artistically inclined members of the earlier committees, who produced a polished drawing of the design. Exactly one week after being tasked with the Seal design, Thomson presented these drawings to the Continental Congress, along with his own written description of the Great Seal (called a blazon), with the bald eagle as the central figure. Congress approved the design the same day, and the Great Seal was a hit. Before long, the eagle took off as a national symbol, and it was everywhere: money, buildings, novelty butter churns—the works.

Not everyone was a fan, however. In a 1784 letter to his daughter, Benjamin Franklin dissed the bald eagle as "a bird of bad moral character," because of its habit of stealing fish from the fishing hawk. He suggested that the turkey would make a better choice, noting, "The turkey is in comparison a much more respectable bird... he is besides (though a little vain and silly, it is true, but not the worse emblem for that) a bird of courage, and would not hesitate to attack a grenadier of the British guards, who should presume to invade his farm yard with a red coat on."

Franklin wasn't entirely serious, of course, but who knows? If he had pitched the idea a few years earlier, we might be known as the fightin' turkeys.

Q: Why do AM stations broadcast farther than FM stations?

A: You're on a long road trip, in the middle of nowhere, scanning the car radio dial for something to keep you awake as you speed through the night. On AM, you pick up a lot of static and some distant station with a guy blathering on and on about taxes or global warming or UFOs or something. You switch over to FM, and much to your delight, you land on a station with crystal-clear reception. It's playing that awesome song that totally takes you back to your senior year of high school, so you rock on. Until about twenty minutes later, when that station begins to fade. You flip back to AM, and there's that annoying guy again, still going strong. You love your radio. Why is it being so cruel to you?

It's not your radio that's being cruel to you—it's the ionosphere. The ionosphere is a layer of the earth's atmosphere that begins about thirty miles above the planet's surface. Ions and electrons in the ionosphere have the ability to reflect radio waves. But not all radio waves. And not all the time.

During the day, the ionosphere has little effect on radio waves. At night, however, the ionosphere acts like a roof. AM radio waves bounce off the ionosphere and bend back down to the surface of the earth. These waves can keep bouncing back and forth like this, sometimes for hundreds of miles, which is why you can hear that faraway AM station and its babbling announcer all night long.

FM radio waves, on the other hand, are largely unaffected by the ionosphere. When an FM station transmits a signal, that signal travels in a straight line until it reaches the horizon as seen from the location and height of the transmitter. The higher the transmitting tower and the farther the visible horizon, the farther the station can be heard. But even the highest towers generally send an FM signal only about fifty miles or so before the signal passes the horizon, snickers at the ionosphere, and heads into the depths of space.

That's where, presumably, a three-headed alien teenager is listening to Boston's "Don't Look Back" for the thousandth time, and his three-headed alien parents are cursing the earthlings who created that noise and are vowing revenge. Consult your radio's AM band for more information on their impending arrival.

Q: Why are we supposed to remember the Alamo?

A: The average three-year-old in Texas can probably tell you about the Alamo, complete with names, dates, and cool sound effects. But it's understandable if the details are a little hazy for the rest of us. We have our own state histories to worry about.

The Alamo began as a Roman Catholic mission called Misión San Antonio de Valero, which was established by the Spanish in the early eighteenth century to convert Native Americans to Christianity. The missionaries moved out in 1793, and nine years later, a Spanish cavalry company moved in, turning it into a fort that it called the Alamo (after Alamo de Parras, the city in Mexico that had been the company's home base). When the Mexican War of Independence ended in 1821, Mexican soldiers had control of all of San Antonio, including the Alamo, and they built up the fort's defenses.

But no one cares if you remember any of this stuff. You're supposed to remember the Alamo because of what happened there during the Texas Revolution. This was a conflict between the Mexican government and the Texians—people who had moved to Mexican territory from the United States. The Texians chafed under the government of Mexican president General Antonio López de Santa Anna Pérez de Lebrón (or Santa Anna to his friends), who was trying to assert more central control over the region. The Texians rebelled against this crackdown and took control of San Antonio and the Alamo, among other places.

On February 23, 1836, General Santa Anna and thousands of soldiers showed up to reclaim the Alamo. William Travis, the commander of the Texian insurgents who held the Alamo, sent messengers out to request help from surrounding communities. He got only thirty-two more volunteers, bringing his fighting force up to about two hundred men. Though they were clearly outnumbered, Travis and his men decided that they would rather die than surrender the fort. They held out for thirteen days, but in a final assault on March 6, Santa Anna's soldiers took control of the fort and killed Travis and all of his men.

The defeat infuriated the Texian revolutionaries and strengthened their resolve. Two months later at the Battle of San Jacinto, Texian soldiers led by General Sam Houston shouted, "Remember the Alamo!" as they charged into the fray. The rebels defeated the Mexican army, captured Santa Anna, and won Texas its independence. "Remember the Alamo!" became a rallying cry, and the battle went down in history as a tale of brave men standing their ground against terrible odds.

The resulting Republic of Texas was short-lived and unstable, thanks in part to continued skirmishes with the Mexican army. On December 29, 1845, Texas became a U.S. state, and it wasn't long before Mexico and the United States were embroiled in the Mexican-American War. But that's another story for another book.

Q: Why does ninety-three octane gas cost more than eighty-seven octane gas?

A: For drivers of a certain age, the call to "fill 'er up with ethyl" conjures memories of gasoline at thirty-two cents a gallon and a high school kid pumping it into your tank, checking the oil, and cleaning your windshield in the bargain. What ethyl buyers were asking for was gasoline dosed with tetraethyl (lead), an additive that kept the fuel in their engine's cylinders from igniting prematurely and damaging the motor.

Gasoline's resistance to premature ignition is reflected in its octane rating—the higher the rating, the greater the resistance. "Ethyl," which had a higher octane rating than "regular" gas, was outlawed in the mid-1970s because its lead component was incompatible with new automotive emissions systems and clean-air standards. However, what was true in the ethyl age is true today: The higher the octane rating, the more expensive the gas.

Octane ratings of eighty-seven for regular grade gas, eighty-nine for mid-grade, and ninety-one to ninety-three for premium are modern standards. The numbers represent a mathematical middle ground between two laboratory tests designed to evaluate an engine's octane requirements under various conditions.

These numbers can also signal a drain on your pocketbook. It isn't unusual for the pump price to jump ten cents per gallon with each octane bump, so ninety-one octane can cost twenty cents more per gallon than eighty-seven octane.

Part of the expense originates at the refinery. Additional processing and costly chemical additives are required to boost octane ratings. Refiners pass these costs along to consumers. Once gas reaches the service station, other factors come into play. High-octane grades account for a small share of fuel sales, but the cost of delivering, storing, and dispensing them is no less than for regular grades. Steeper pump prices help service stations recoup some of that uneven overhead.

And don't overlook good old profit-padding. Retailers charge more for premium gas because they can. They market higher-octane gas to drivers of luxury vehicles or sporty cars with performance-tuned engines. Automakers recommend—and in some cases, require—that some models take fuel with an octane rating of eighty-nine or higher.

High-performance engines need fuel that burns slower, not quicker. Basically, they get more bang for each burn of the air-fuel mixture within the combustion chamber. That breeds levels of heat and pressure that promote premature ignition.

Premature ignition is bad for any engine. We're talking milliseconds, but if the air-fuel mixture in the combustion chamber begins to burn just before the spark plug ignites it, the result is a double dose of detonation that knocks back the piston with exceptional force. In fact, it makes a knocking sound. That's why octane-enhancing additives are called anti-knock agents. Subject any engine to enough knocking, and you'll be in for a big repair bill.

The good news is that most cars are designed for eighty-seven octane gas. Check your owner's manual and follow the manufacturer's octane advice. Using a higher-octane gas than recommended won't increase gas mileage or make your engine run any smoother, so don't pay for octane you don't need, especially in this age of obscene gas prices.

Contributors

Brett Ballantini is a sportswriter who has written for several major sports teams and has authored a book titled *The Wit and Wisdom of Ozzie Guillen*.

Diane Lanzillotta Bobis is a food, fashion, and lifestyle writer from Glenview, Illinois.

Joshua D. Boeringa is a writer living in Mt. Pleasant, Michigan. He has written for magazines and Web sites.

Anthony G. Craine is a contributor to the *Britannica Book of the Year* and has written for magazines including *Inside Sports* and *Ask*. He is a former United Press International bureau chief.

Dan Dalton is a writer and editor who hails from Michigan.

Shanna Freeman is a writer and editor living near Atlanta. She also works in an academic library.

Chuck Giametta is a highly acclaimed journalist who specializes in coverage of the automotive industry. He has written and edited books, magazines, and Web articles on a number of automotive topics.

Ed Grabianowski writes about science and nature, history, the automotive industry, and science fiction for Web sites and magazines. He lives in Buffalo, New York.

Jack Greer is a writer living in Chicago.

Tom Harris is a Web project consultant, and editor. He is the cofounder of Explainist.com and was leader of the editorial content team at HowStuffWorks.com.

Vickey Kalambakal is a writer and historian based in Southern California. She writes for textbooks, encyclopedias, magazines, and ezines.

Brett Kyle is a writer living in Draycott, Somerset, England. He also is an actor, musician, singer, and playwright.

Noah Liberman is a Chicago-based sports, entertainment, and business writer who has published two books and has contributed articles to a wide range of newspapers and national magazines.

Letty Livingston is a dating coach and relationship counselor.

Alex Nechas is a writer and editor based in Chicago.

Jessica Royer Ocken is a freelance writer and editor based in Chicago.

Thad Plumley is an award-winning writer who lives in Dublin, Ohio. He is the director of publications and information products for the National Ground Water Association.

Pat Sherman is a writer living in Cambridge, Massachusetts. She is the author several books for children, including *The Sun's Daughter* and *Ben and the Proclamation of Emancipation*.

Carrie Williford is a writer living in Atlanta. She was a contributing writer to HowStuffWorks.com.

Factual verification: Darcy Chadwick, Barbara Cross, Bonny M. Davidson, Andrew Garrett, Cindy Hangartner, Brenda McLean, Carl Miller, Katrina O'Brien, Marilyn Perlberg